Basic Computation

Quizzes and Tests

Loretta M. Taylor, Ed. D.
Mathematics Teacher
Hillsdale High School
San Mateo, California

Harold D. Taylor, Ed. D.
Head, Mathematics Department
Aragon High School
San Mateo, California

DALE
SEYMOUR
PUBLICATIONS
P.O. BOX 10888
PALO ALTO, CA 94303

Editors: Elaine C. Murphy, Susan McCalla
Production Coordinator: Ruth Cottrell
Cover designer: Michael Rogondino
Technical Art: Pat Rogondino
Compositor: WB Associates
Printer: Malloy Lithographing

ISBN 0-86651-009-5

Catalog number DS01190

11 12 13 14 15 -MA- 99 98 97

DALE
SEYMOUR
PUBLICATIONS
P.O. BOX 10888
PALO ALTO, CA 94303

ABOUT THE PROGRAM

WHAT IS THE BASIC COMPUTATION LIBRARY?

The books in the BASIC COMPUTATION library together provide comprehensive practice in all the essential computational skills. There are practice books and a test book. The practice books consist of carefully sequenced drill worksheets organized in groups of five. The test book contains daily quizzes (160 quizzes in all), semester tests, and year-end tests written in standardized-test formats.

If you find this book effective, you may want to use others in the series. Build your own library to suit your own needs.

BOOK 1	WORKING WITH WHOLE NUMBERS
BOOK 2	UNDERSTANDING FRACTIONS
BOOK 3	WORKING WITH FRACTIONS
BOOK 4	WORKING WITH DECIMALS
BOOK 5	WORKING WITH PERCENTS
BOOK 6	UNDERSTANDING MEASUREMENT
BOOK 7	FINDING AREA AND PERIMETER
BOOK 8	WORKING WITH CIRCLES AND VOLUME
BOOK 9	APPLYING COMPUTATIONAL SKILLS
TEST BOOK	BASIC COMPUTATION QUIZZES AND TESTS

WHO CAN USE THE BASIC COMPUTATION LIBRARY?

Classroom teachers, substitute teachers, tutors, parents, and persons wishing to study on their own can use these materials. Although written specifically for the general math classroom, books in the BASIC COMPUTATION library can be used with any program requiring carefully sequenced computational practice. The material is appropriate for use with any person, young or old, who has not yet certified computational proficiency. It is especially suitable for middle school, junior high school, and high school students who need to master the essential computational skills necessary for mathematical literacy.

WHAT IS IN THIS BOOK?

This book is a test book. In addition to these teacher notes, it contains student quizzes, two first-semester tests, two year-end tests, and response forms.

Quizzes

The quizzes are designed to give teachers the opportunity to check up on students' skills. Each quiz comes in four equivalent forms allowing for four daily quizzes a week. There are 40 weeks of quizzes, 160 quizzes in all. Each quiz provides exercises in only one or two specific skills. Instructions are clear and simple. There are enough problems to give teachers the opportunity to diagnose student errors and few enough for the quizzes to take only a short period of time. The answer to each problem is included in the back of this book.

Tests

The tests provide questions on all the essential computational skills measured on competency tests. There are two 100-question first-semester tests and two 100-question year-end tests, all written in standard multiple-choice format. The tests can be used as final exams for each semester, as practice for final exams, or as practice for minimal competency tests. The answer to each problem is included in the back of this book.

Response Form

A response form similar to those used with standardized tests is provided for use with the tests.

Answers

Answers to each problem are included in the back of the book.

HOW CAN THE BASIC COMPUTATION LIBRARY BE USED?

The materials in the BASIC COMPUTATION library can serve as the major skeleton of a skills program or as supplements to any other computational skills program. The large number of worksheets gives a wide variety from which to choose and allows flexibility in structuring a program to meet individual needs. The following suggestions are offered to show how the BASIC COMPUTATION library may be adapted to a particular situation.

Minimal Competency Practice

In various fields and schools, standardized tests are used for entrance, passage from one level to another, and certification of competency or proficiency prior to graduation. The materials in the BASIC COMPUTATION library are particularly well-suited to preparing for any of the various mathematics competency tests, including the mathematics portion of the General Educational Development test (GED) used to certify high school equivalency.

Together, the books in the BASIC COMPUTATION library give practice in all the essential computational skills measured on competency tests. The semester tests and year-end tests from the test book are written in standardized-test formats. These tests can be used as sample minimal competency tests. The worksheets can be used to brush up on skills measured by the competency tests. The quizzes can be used to check up on previously studied skills.

Skill Maintenance

The quizzes come in four equivalent forms. They can be used each day for maintenance of previously-learned skills or diagnosis of skill deficiencies. Used along with the daily worksheets from the other books in the BASIC COMPUTATION library, they provide either warm-up or check-up activities for each day's work.

The tests can be used at the end of each semester as final exams. Since there are two forms for each test, one form could be used for review and the other form for the examination.

Supplementary Drill

There are more than 18,000 problems in the BASIC COMPUTATION library. When students need more practice with a given skill, use the appropriate quizzes and worksheets from the library. They are suitable for classwork or homework practice following the teaching of a specific skill. With four equivalent pages for each quiz and five equivalent pages for most worksheets, adequate practice is provided for each essential skill.

HOW ARE MATERIALS PREPARED?

The books are designed so the pages can be easily removed and reproduced by Thermofax, Xerox, or a similar process. For example, a ditto master can be made on a Thermofax for use on a spirit duplicator. Permanent transparencies can be made by processing special transparencies through a Thermofax or Xerox.

Any system will run more smoothly if work is stored in folders. Record forms can be attached to the folders so that either students or teachers can keep records of individual progress. Materials stored in this way are readily available for conferences.

The multiple-choice format of the semester- and year-end tests allows you to grade quickly with a Scantron if one is available.

Exam   Name _____

                              Date _____

1. A B C D	26. A B C D	51. A B C D	76. A B C D
2. A B C D	27. A B C D	52. A B C D	77. A B C D
3. A B C D	28. A B C D	53. A B C D	78. A B C D
4. A B C D	29. A B C D	54. A B C D	79. A B C D
5. A B C D	30. A B C D	55. A B C D	80. A B C D
6. A B C D	31. A B C D	56. A B C D	81. A B C D
7. A B C D	32. A B C D	57. A B C D	82. A B C D
8. A B C D	33. A B C D	58. A B C D	83. A B C D
9. A B C D	34. A B C D	59. A B C D	84. A B C D
10. A B C D	35. A B C D	60. A B C D	85. A B C D
11. A B C D	36. A B C D	61. A B C D	86. A B C D
12. A B C D	37. A B C D	62. A B C D	87. A B C D
13. A B C D	38. A B C D	63. A B C D	88. A B C D
14. A B C D	39. A B C D	64. A B C D	89. A B C D
15. A B C D	40. A B C D	65. A B C D	90. A B C D
16. A B C D	41. A B C D	66. A B C D	91. A B C D
17. A B C D	42. A B C D	67. A B C D	92. A B C D
18. A B C D	43. A B C D	68. A B C D	93. A B C D
19. A B C D	44. A B C D	69. A B C D	94. A B C D
20. A B C D	45. A B C D	70. A B C D	95. A B C D
21. A B C D	46. A B C D	71. A B C D	96. A B C D
22. A B C D	47. A B C D	72. A B C D	97. A B C D
23. A B C D	48. A B C D	73. A B C D	98. A B C D
24. A B C D	49. A B C D	74. A B C D	99. A B C D
25. A B C D	50. A B C D	75. A B C D	100. A B C D

Quiz

Addition of whole numbers

Name _____

Date _____

Find each sum.

1.   5
    3
    6
    9
 +8
	2. 423,987
	 + 27,854
		3. Find the sum of 9, 58, and 725.

4.   15
     79
      3
   874
+ 72
	5. 73
	    57
	    49
	 +21
		6. $29 + 83 + 47 = ?$

7. Find the sum of 387, 425, and 478.	**8.** $49 + 1302 + 84 = ?$	**9.** 876
		    14,247
		       900
		+7,003,468

10.   5473
     439
    6347
 + 246
	11. Find the sum of 27,867 and 946.	**12.** 7,395,460
		    672,008
		+45,538,475

13. Find the sum of 407,083, 39, and 575.	**14.** 10,457
	  206,003
	      290
	   4,580
	+ 72,342
		15. $561 + 27 + 303 = ?$

Name _____

Date _____

Find each sum.

1.   6
           5
           9
           4
      +7
	2. 637,495
	   + 46,887
		3. Find the sum of 7, 95, and 823.

4.   15
        72
          8
     946
   + 74
	5. 73
	       75
	       46
	       29
	    +37
		6. $25 + 73 + 48 = ?$

7. Find the sum of 583, 217, and 423.	**8.** $43 + 1506 + 96 = ?$	**9.** 875
		    14,372
		       900
		  +700,893

10.   4396
      297
    8625
   + 263
	11. Find the sum of 37,854 and 972.	**12.** 8,395,680
		     748,005
		  +41,568,337

13. Find the sum of 506,842, 73, and 592.	**14.** 10,638
	   307,004
	       297
	     4,845
	  + 57,250
		15. $472 + 27 + 506 = ?$

Quiz

Addition of whole numbers

Name _____

Date _____

Find each sum.

1.   5
    7
    9
    3
+8
	2. 538,427
	+ 95,374
		3. Find the sum of 8, 47, and 764.

4.   18
    63
     9
  431
+ 87
	5. 93
	    65
	    82
	    43
	+52
		6. 46 + 82 + 73 = ?

7. Find the sum of 272, 583, and 921.	**8.** 62 + 1307 + 48 = ?	**9.** 672
		   23,557
		     800
		+800,853

10.   3827
   934
  5956
+ 732
	11. Find the sum of 43,781 and 856.	**12.** 8,976,314
		   825,503
		+68,843,705

13. Find the sum of 807,463, 29, and 482.	**14.** 20,533
	 609,004
	    368
	  6,965
	+ 38,544
		15. 352 + 72 + 804 = ?

3

Name _____

Date _____

Find each sum.

1.   9
         8
         7
         2
     +4
	2. 384,762
	   + 58,773
		3. Find the sum of 7, 64, and 823.

4.   26
      93
       8
    772
  + 83
	5. 54
	     47
	     63
	  +51
		6. 38 + 52 + 69 = ?

7. Find the sum of 548, 821, and 694.	**8.** 86 + 1407 + 92 = ?	**9.** 436
		     15,762
		       800
		 +8,005,937

10.   8327
    631
   5357
 + 462
	11. Find the sum of 59,473 and 968.	**12.** 8,359,281
		    697,006
		 +59,463,227

13. Find the sum of 907,035, 53, and 281.	**14.** 20,674
	  357,963
	     340
	   3,690
	 + 58,731
		15. 895 + 36 + 404 = ?

Quiz

Subtraction of whole numbers

Name _____

Date _____

Find each difference.

1. 469 − 95	**2.** 486 − 85 = ?	**3.** 71,003 − 1,596
4. Find the difference between 5837 and 712.	**5.** 8854 − 895	**6.** Subtract 94 from 736.
7. What number is 41 less than 600?	**8.** 575 − 136 = ?	**9.** Find the difference between 583 and 795.
10. 15,876 − 12,482 = ?	**11.** 50,903 − 4,726	**12.** 813,230 − 97,538
13. 7132 is how much more than 3567?	**14.** Subtract 436 from 862.	**15.** 703,624 − 999 = ?

Name _____

Date _____

Find each difference.

1.   694
     − 372
	2. 268 − 94 = ?	**3.** 46,993
		     − 735

4. Find the difference between 974 and 385.	**5.** 45,139 − 8,457	**6.** Subtract 63 from 97.
7. Subtract 247 from 314.	**8.** 274 − 75 = ?	**9.** Find the difference between 549 and 827.

10.   69,470
     − 398
	11. 90,048
	     − 6,095
		12. 493,094
		     − 38,245

13. 2793 is how much more than 2489?	**14.** Subtract 394 from 2356.	**15.** 540,027 − 595 = ?

Name _____

Date _____

Find each difference.

1. 87,463 − 6,292	**2.** Subtract 6389 from 7499.	**3.** 43,521 − 37,483 = ?
4. Subtract 478 from 15,620.	**5.** 55,555 − 39,586	**6.** 972 − 499 = ?
7. Subtract 15,791 from 24,650.	**8.** 75,643 − 9822 = ?	**9.** Subtract 1668 from 3577.
10. 12,345 − 6,789	**11.** 25,371 − 19,850 = ?	**12.** Subtract 3333 from 12,121.
13. Subtract 189 from 240.	**14.** 53,520 − 47,631	**15.** 50,403 − 3,624 = ?

Quiz

Subtraction of whole numbers

Name _____

Date _____

Find each difference.

1. 69,235 − 8,316	**2.** Subtract 9325 from 18,330.	**3.** 92,351 − 26,538 = ?
4. Subtract 947 from 26,830.	**5.** 66,666 − 48,789	**6.** 887 − 388 = ?
7. Subtract 35,612 from 57,431.	**8.** 13,976 − 8732 = ?	**9.** Subtract 1792 from 4699.
10. 31,426 − 7,839	**11.** 35,816 − 13,720 = ?	**12.** Subtract 2222 from 31,313.
13. Subtract 159 from 360.	**14.** 73,750 − 56,241	**15.** 60,702 − 4634 = ?

Quiz

Multiplication by one-digit numbers

Name _____

Date _____

Find each product.

1. $\begin{array}{r} 12 \\ \times\ \ 7 \\ \hline \end{array}$	**2.** $\begin{array}{r} 342 \\ \times\ \ \ 8 \\ \hline \end{array}$	**3.** $\begin{array}{r} 783 \\ \times\ \ \ 4 \\ \hline \end{array}$
4. $\begin{array}{r} 596 \\ \times\ \ \ 3 \\ \hline \end{array}$	**5.** $\begin{array}{r} 843 \\ \times\ \ \ 5 \\ \hline \end{array}$	**6.** $\begin{array}{r} 1396 \\ \times\ \ \ \ 6 \\ \hline \end{array}$
7. $\begin{array}{r} 348 \\ \times\ \ \ 2 \\ \hline \end{array}$	**8.** $\begin{array}{r} 513 \\ \times\ \ \ 9 \\ \hline \end{array}$	**9.** $\begin{array}{r} 524 \\ \times\ \ \ 8 \\ \hline \end{array}$
10. $\begin{array}{r} 678 \\ \times\ \ \ 3 \\ \hline \end{array}$	**11.** $\begin{array}{r} 403 \\ \times\ \ \ 4 \\ \hline \end{array}$	**12.** $\begin{array}{r} 589 \\ \times\ \ \ 1 \\ \hline \end{array}$

Quiz

Multiplication by one-digit numbers

Name _____

Date _____

Find each product.

1. $\begin{array}{r} 15 \\ \times\ 3 \\ \hline \end{array}$	**2.** $\begin{array}{r} 24 \\ \times\ 5 \\ \hline \end{array}$	**3.** $\begin{array}{r} 18 \\ \times\ 6 \\ \hline \end{array}$
4. $\begin{array}{r} 36 \\ \times\ 7 \\ \hline \end{array}$	**5.** $\begin{array}{r} 47 \\ \times\ 8 \\ \hline \end{array}$	**6.** $\begin{array}{r} 29 \\ \times\ 9 \\ \hline \end{array}$
7. $\begin{array}{r} 739 \\ \times\ 3 \\ \hline \end{array}$	**8.** $\begin{array}{r} 587 \\ \times\ 9 \\ \hline \end{array}$	**9.** $\begin{array}{r} 138 \\ \times\ 6 \\ \hline \end{array}$
10. $\begin{array}{r} 597 \\ \times\ 5 \\ \hline \end{array}$	**11.** $\begin{array}{r} 843 \\ \times\ 7 \\ \hline \end{array}$	**12.** $\begin{array}{r} 1436 \\ \times\ 8 \\ \hline \end{array}$

Name _____

Date _____

Find each product.

1.   51
     × 2
	2. 40
	     × 4
		3. 29
		     × 1

4.   54
     × 6
	5. 98
	     × 3
		6. 36
		     × 5

7.   40
     × 2
	8. 81
	     × 3
		9. 49
		     × 6

10.   153
      × 9
	11. 267
	      × 8
		12. 348
		      × 7

Quiz
Multiplication by one-digit numbers

Name _____

Date _____

Find each product.

1. 27 $\times$ 1	**2.** 98 $\times$ 4	**3.** 69 $\times$ 5
4. 20 $\times$ 7	**5.** 36 $\times$ 9	**6.** 35 $\times$ 8
7. 15 $\times$ 7	**8.** 67 $\times$ 9	**9.** 53 $\times$ 7
10. 860 $\times$ 9	**11.** 571 $\times$ 9	**12.** 136 $\times$ 6

Quiz

Multiplication by two-digit numbers

Name _____

Date _____

Find each product.

1.   15
    × 12
	2. 24
	    × 35
		3. 10
		    × 16

4.   84
    × 47
	5. 98
	    × 15
		6. 44
		    × 89

7.   129
    ×   10
	8. 293
	    × 23
		9. 402
		    × 67

10.   276
    ×   45
	11. 345
	    × 81
		12. 782
		    × 96

Quiz

Multiplication by two-digit numbers

Name _____

Date _____

Find each product.

1.   17
    × 35
	2. 18
	    × 40
		3. 76
		    × 29

4.   84
    × 37
	5. 20
	    × 16
		6. 59
		    × 31

7.   462
    × 38
	8. 79
	    × 52
		9. 146
		    × 85

10.   237
    × 91
	11. 420
	    × 64
		12. 508
		    × 83

14

Quiz

Multiplication by two-digit numbers

Name _____

Date _____

Find each product.

1.   43
      × 25
	2. 16
	      × 70
		3. 89
		      × 26

4.   57
      × 13
	5. 48
	      × 91
		6. 40
		      × 13

7.   253
      × 36
	8. 348
	      × 94
		9. 149
		      × 38

10.   256
      × 73
	11. 407
	      × 98
		12. 126
		      × 35

Quiz

Multiplication by two-digit numbers

Name _____

Date _____

Find each product.

1. $\begin{array}{r} 47 \\ \times\,20 \\ \hline \end{array}$	2. $\begin{array}{r} 26 \\ \times\,18 \\ \hline \end{array}$	3. $\begin{array}{r} 20 \\ \times\,45 \\ \hline \end{array}$
4. $\begin{array}{r} 26 \\ \times\,34 \\ \hline \end{array}$	5. $\begin{array}{r} 75 \\ \times\,93 \\ \hline \end{array}$	6. $\begin{array}{r} 82 \\ \times\,15 \\ \hline \end{array}$
7. $\begin{array}{r} 618 \\ \times\,\ 55 \\ \hline \end{array}$	8. $\begin{array}{r} 523 \\ \times\,\ 72 \\ \hline \end{array}$	9. $\begin{array}{r} 734 \\ \times\,\ 93 \\ \hline \end{array}$
10. $\begin{array}{r} 256 \\ \times\,\ 60 \\ \hline \end{array}$	11. $\begin{array}{r} 728 \\ \times\,\ 29 \\ \hline \end{array}$	12. $\begin{array}{r} 375 \\ \times\,\ 71 \\ \hline \end{array}$

Multiplication of whole numbers

Name _____

Date _____

Find each product.

1. $\begin{array}{r} 2705 \\ \times\quad 9 \\ \hline \end{array}$	**2.** Multiply 47 by 76.	**3.** $\begin{array}{r} 7334 \\ \times\quad 35 \\ \hline \end{array}$
4. $39 \times 54 = ?$	**5.** $\begin{array}{r} 243 \\ \times\ 307 \\ \hline \end{array}$	**6.** Find the product of 73 and 28.
7. $37 \times 12 \times 4 = ?$	**8.** Multiply 89 by 137.	**9.** $43 \times 11 \times 0 = ?$
10. $76 \times 9 = ?$	**11.** $\begin{array}{r} 280,034 \\ \times\quad 3007 \\ \hline \end{array}$	**12.** Find the product of 17 and 23.

Name _____

Date _____

Find each product.

1. 3476 × 27	**2.** Multiply 93 by 48.	**3.** 9999 × 406
4. 68 × 27 = ?	**5.** 176 × 437	**6.** Find the product of 37 and 89.
7. 16 × 27 × 11 = ?	**8.** 8273 × 4009	**9.** 19 × 57 = ?
10. 15 × 25 = ?	**11.** 17 × 23 × 4 = ?	**12.** Find the product of 14 and 12.

Quiz

Multiplication of whole numbers

Name _____

Date _____

Find each product.

1. 7382 $\times$ 8	2. Multiply 83 by 27.	3. 5863 $\times$ 45
4. $37 \times 63 = ?$	5. 407 $\times$ 206	6. Find the product of 137 and 14.
7. $43 \times 35 \times 3 = ?$	8. Multiply 53 by 172.	9. $85 \times 0 \times 592 = ?$
10. $55 \times 7 = ?$	11. 583,630 $\times$ 5072	12. Find the product of 24 and 16.

Quiz

Multiplication of whole numbers

Name _____

Date _____

Find each product.

1.   6922
      ×   8
	2. Multiply 39 by 14.	**3.** 5607
		     × 67

4. $59 \times 37 = ?$	**5.** 702 × 601	**6.** Find the product of 92 and 46.
7. $17 \times 28 \times 3 = ?$	**8.** Multiply 37 by 2745.	**9.** $0 \times 62 \times 71 = ?$
10. $427 \times 8 = ?$	**11.** 621,314 × 8025	**12.** Find the product of 42 and 18.

Name _____

Date _____

Find each quotient.

1. 63 ÷ 7 = ?	**2.** 48 ÷ 8 = ?	**3.** 35 ÷ 5 = ?
4. 0 ÷ 5 = ?	**5.** 8 ÷ 1 = ?	**6.** 24 ÷ 3 = ?
7. 54 ÷ 6 = ?	**8.** 56 ÷ 7 = ?	**9.** 42 ÷ 6 = ?
10. 25 ÷ 5 = ?	**11.** 21 ÷ 7 = ?	**12.** 21 ÷ 3 = ?
13. 50 ÷ 5 = ?	**14.** 72 ÷ 9 = ?	**15.** 81 ÷ 9 = ?
16. 30 ÷ 6 = ?	**17.** 28 ÷ 7 = ?	**18.** 40 ÷ 8 = ?
19. 27 ÷ 9 = ?	**20.** 60 ÷ 10 = ?	**21.** 100 ÷ 10 = ?
22. 24 ÷ 6 = ?	**23.** 36 ÷ 6 = ?	**24.** 32 ÷ 8 = ?
25. 64 ÷ 8 = ?	**26.** 18 ÷ 3 = ?	**27.** 70 ÷ 10 = ?
28. 20 ÷ 4 = ?	**29.** 0 ÷ 10 = ?	**30.** 18 ÷ 9 = ?

Quiz

Division by one-digit numbers

Name _____

Date _____

Find each quotient and remainder.

1. $26 \div 3 = ?$	**2.** $17 \div 2 = ?$	**3.** $29 \div 4 = ?$
4. $58 \div 7 = ?$	**5.** $1 \div 2 = ?$	**6.** $31 \div 4 = ?$
7. $23 \div 4 = ?$	**8.** $20 \div 3 = ?$	**9.** $9 \div 2 = ?$
10. $60 \div 9 = ?$	**11.** $50 \div 8 = ?$	**12.** $33 \div 5 = ?$
13. $39 \div 8 = ?$	**14.** $27 \div 4 = ?$	**15.** $19 \div 3 = ?$
16. $42 \div 5 = ?$	**17.** $56 \div 6 = ?$	**18.** $83 \div 9 = ?$
19. $61 \div 8 = ?$	**20.** $54 \div 7 = ?$	**21.** $32 \div 6 = ?$
22. $43 \div 5 = ?$	**23.** $39 \div 9 = ?$	**24.** $54 \div 7 = ?$
25. $26 \div 3 = ?$	**26.** $57 \div 7 = ?$	**27.** $49 \div 8 = ?$
28. $30 \div 9 = ?$	**29.** $67 \div 8 = ?$	**30.** $19 \div 2 = ?$

Quiz

Division by one-digit numbers

Name _____

Date _____

Find each quotient and remainder.

1. $7 \div 2 = ?$	**2.** $14 \div 6 = ?$	**3.** $29 \div 4 = ?$
4. $57 \div 9 = ?$	**5.** $43 \div 6 = ?$	**6.** $36 \div 8 = ?$
7. $13 \div 2 = ?$	**8.** $34 \div 6 = ?$	**9.** $27 \div 4 = ?$
10. $45 \div 6 = ?$	**11.** $27 \div 4 = ?$	**12.** $38 \div 5 = ?$
13. $23 \div 3 = ?$	**14.** $61 \div 9 = ?$	**15.** $15 \div 2 = ?$
16. $34 \div 7 = ?$	**17.** $29 \div 9 = ?$	**18.** $16 \div 3 = ?$
19. $36 \div 8 = ?$	**20.** $51 \div 7 = ?$	**21.** $23 \div 5 = ?$
22. $48 \div 7 = ?$	**23.** $29 \div 8 = ?$	**24.** $21 \div 9 = ?$
25. $33 \div 4 = ?$	**26.** $61 \div 8 = ?$	**27.** $25 \div 3 = ?$
28. $15 \div 2 = ?$	**29.** $17 \div 5 = ?$	**30.** $29 \div 3 = ?$

Quiz
Division by one-digit numbers

Name _____

Date _____

Find each quotient and remainder.

1. $39 \div 4 = ?$	**2.** $60 \div 9 = ?$	**3.** $39 \div 9 = ?$
4. $51 \div 9 = ?$	**5.** $17 \div 2 = ?$	**6.** $33 \div 4 = ?$
7. $27 \div 7 = ?$	**8.** $39 \div 7 = ?$	**9.** $47 \div 8 = ?$
10. $28 \div 8 = ?$	**11.** $43 \div 9 = ?$	**12.** $26 \div 3 = ?$
13. $13 \div 2 = ?$	**14.** $20 \div 3 = ?$	**15.** $11 \div 2 = ?$
16. $19 \div 6 = ?$	**17.** $20 \div 8 = ?$	**18.** $32 \div 5 = ?$
19. $17 \div 4 = ?$	**20.** $20 \div 7 = ?$	**21.** $16 \div 3 = ?$
22. $20 \div 6 = ?$	**23.** $27 \div 5 = ?$	**24.** $7 \div 2 = ?$
25. $33 \div 4 = ?$	**26.** $30 \div 7 = ?$	**27.** $35 \div 6 = ?$
28. $28 \div 5 = ?$	**29.** $60 \div 8 = ?$	**30.** $17 \div 3 = ?$

Quiz

Division by two-digit numbers

Name _____

Date _____

Find each quotient.

1. 1302 ÷ 31 = ?	**2.** 1368 ÷ 72 = ?	**3.** 4048 ÷ 44 = ?
4. 1971 ÷ 73 = ?	**5.** 3904 ÷ 64 = ?	**6.** 3649 ÷ 41 = ?
7. 2144 ÷ 32 = ?	**8.** 1183 ÷ 13 = ?	**9.** 4221 ÷ 63 = ?
10. 4664 ÷ 53 = ?	**11.** 2170 ÷ 70 = ?	**12.** 8178 ÷ 94 = ?

Name _____

Date _____

Find each quotient.

1. 924 ÷ 12 = ?	**2.** 5340 ÷ 60 = ?	**3.** 1173 ÷ 51 = ?
4. 3358 ÷ 73 = ?	**5.** 1248 ÷ 24 = ?	**6.** 6532 ÷ 92 = ?
7. 1517 ÷ 41 = ?	**8.** 3604 ÷ 53 = ?	**9.** 2241 ÷ 83 = ?
10. 3200 ÷ 64 = ?	**11.** 5976 ÷ 72 = ?	**12.** 3479 ÷ 71 = ?

Quiz

Name _____

Division by two-digit numbers

Date _____

Find each quotient.

1. $3551 \div 53 = ?$	**2.** $2116 \div 92 = ?$	**3.** $3478 \div 74 = ?$
4. $2916 \div 81 = ?$	**5.** $4544 \div 64 = ?$	**6.** $928 \div 32 = ?$
7. $1027 \div 13 = ?$	**8.** $2132 \div 41 = ?$	**9.** $2697 \div 93 = ?$
10. $2508 \div 44 = ?$	**11.** $3276 \div 52 = ?$	**12.** $1302 \div 31 = ?$

Name _____

Date _____

Find each quotient.

1. 4819 ÷ 61 = ?	**2.** 3564 ÷ 44 = ?	**3.** 4232 ÷ 92 = ?
4. 828 ÷ 23 = ?	**5.** 1728 ÷ 72 = ?	**6.** 1079 ÷ 13 = ?
7. 2268 ÷ 54 = ?	**8.** 7600 ÷ 80 = ?	**9.** 2738 ÷ 74 = ?
10. 5208 ÷ 93 = ?	**11.** 756 ÷ 12 = ?	**12.** 600 ÷ 24 = ?

Quiz

More division by two-digit numbers

Name _____

Date _____

Find each quotient.

1. 1856 ÷ 64 = ?	**2.** 1908 ÷ 53 = ?	**3.** 1512 ÷ 21 = ?
4. 5428 ÷ 92 = ?	**5.** 4824 ÷ 72 = ?	**6.** 3483 ÷ 81 = ?
7. 1118 ÷ 43 = ?	**8.** 510 ÷ 30 = ?	**9.** 812 ÷ 14 = ?
10. 2870 ÷ 82 = ?	**11.** 4914 ÷ 63 = ?	**12.** 6097 ÷ 91 = ?

Quiz
More division by two-digit numbers

Name _____

Date _____

Find each quotient.

1. 414 ÷ 18 = ?	**2.** 782 ÷ 46 = ?	**3.** 928 ÷ 29 = ?
4. 2993 ÷ 73 = ?	**5.** 1472 ÷ 16 = ?	**6.** 2491 ÷ 53 = ?
7. 832 ÷ 26 = ?	**8.** 2726 ÷ 47 = ?	**9.** 2745 ÷ 61 = ?
10. 1456 ÷ 28 = ?	**11.** 2747 ÷ 67 = ?	**12.** 2484 ÷ 92 = ?

Quiz

More division by two-digit numbers

Name _____

Date _____

Find each quotient.

1. 756 ÷ 36 = ?	**2.** 2544 ÷ 53 = ?	**3.** 594 ÷ 27 = ?
4. 656 ÷ 16 = ?	**5.** 480 ÷ 15 = ?	**6.** 555 ÷ 37 = ?
7. 1118 ÷ 43 = ?	**8.** 4524 ÷ 87 = ?	**9.** 462 ÷ 33 = ?
10. 1550 ÷ 25 = ?	**11.** 1701 ÷ 63 = ?	**12.** 2592 ÷ 81 = ?

Quiz

More division by two-digit numbers

Name _____

Date _____

Find each quotient.

1. 1548 ÷ 36 = ?	**2.** 2448 ÷ 48 = ?	**3.** 784 ÷ 16 = ?
4. 396 ÷ 18 = ?	**5.** 1081 ÷ 23 = ?	**6.** 528 ÷ 16 = ?
7. 1326 ÷ 26 = ?	**8.** 2112 ÷ 48 = ?	**9.** 1888 ÷ 59 = ?
10. 2795 ÷ 65 = ?	**11.** 1232 ÷ 77 = ?	**12.** 1911 ÷ 91 = ?

Quiz

Division of whole numbers

Name _____

Date _____

Find each quotient.

1. $488 \div 8 = ?$	**2.** Divide 10,472 by 68.	**3.** $304 \div 76 = ?$
4. $7\overline{)336}$	**5.** $9825 \div 75 = ?$	**6.** Divide 392 by 49.
7. $\dfrac{1260}{18} = ?$	**8.** $65\overline{)22{,}555}$	**9.** $30{,}000 \div 100 = ?$
10. $28 \div 4 = ?$	**11.** Divide 600 by 25.	**12.** $2{,}041{,}600 \div 2900 = ?$

Name _____

Date _____

Find each quotient.

1. $297 \div 3 = ?$	**2.** Divide 47 into 987.	**3.** Divide 486,234 by 6.
4. $\dfrac{292}{146} = ?$	**5.** $299 \div 13 = ?$	**6.** Divide 17,046 by 2841.
7. Divide 1488 by 62.	**8.** $882 \div 14 = ?$	**9.** $1000 \div 10 = ?$
10. $119 \div 7 = ?$	**11.** Divide 169 by 13.	**12.** $1,753,944 \div 5464 = ?$

Quiz

Division of whole numbers

Name _____

Date _____

Find each quotient.

1. $477 \div 9 = ?$	**2.** Divide 8112 by 48.	**3.** $9612 \div 54 = ?$
4. $52\overline{)13{,}104}$	**5.** $209{,}032 \div 8 = ?$	**6.** $10{,}000 \div 1000 = ?$
7. Divide 43 into 1763.	**8.** $62{,}500 \div 2500 = ?$	**9.** $13{,}104 \div 52 = ?$
10. $279 \div 9 = ?$	**11.** Divide 235 by 5.	**12.** $16{,}440{,}321 \div 4107 = ?$

35

Quiz

Division of whole numbers

Name _____

Date _____

Find each quotient.

1. $322 \div 14 = ?$	2. Divide 9922 by 22.	3. Divide 42 into 9198.
4. $35\overline{)2275}$	5. $14{,}432 \div 41 = ?$	6. Divide 4250 by 125.
7. $49{,}686 \div 91 = ?$	8. $212\overline{)14{,}628}$	9. Divide 141,414 by 14.
10. $81 \div 27 = ?$	11. Divide 22,016 by 43.	12. $9200 \div 200 = ?$

Quiz

Review of whole numbers

Name _____

Date _____

Find each sum, difference, product, and quotient.

1.   67
     54
     96
     42
   + 38
	2. 297,012
	 + 874,263
		3. 263
		    821
		    998
		 + 516

4. 507,711 − 89,733	**5.** 410,558 − 273,669	**6.** 401,003 − 272,854
7. 29 × 84	**8.** 587 × 375	**9.** 25,049 × 8221
10. 42)‾25,746	**11.** 803)‾452,892	**12.** 58)‾174,290

Name _____

Date _____

Find each sum, difference, product, and quotient.

1. 26 87 95 42 + 23	**2.** 376,214 + 842,615	**3.** 816 759 426 + 115
4. 807,553 − 49,675	**5.** 786,917 − 497,028	**6.** 700,597 − 492,618
7. 67 × 48	**8.** 867 × 385	**9.** 27,067 × 4002
10. 73)66,357	**11.** 711)154,287	**12.** 97)877,268

Quiz

Review of whole numbers

Name _____

Date _____

Find each sum, difference, product, and quotient.

1.   27
      62
      39
      86
   + 25
	2. 784,309
	  + 873,086
		3. 721
		    132
		    547
		  + 614

4.   804,712
  − 76,538
	5. 386,207
	  − 367,319
		6. 908,043
		  − 259,476

7.   44
  × 29
	8. 862
	  × 258
		9. 43,705
		  × 8002

10. 27)2187	**11.** 307)127,098	**12.** 94)282,470

39

Quiz

Review of whole numbers

Name _____

Date _____

Find each sum, difference, product, and quotient.

1.   43
        72
        69
        57
    + 32
	2. 398,205
	    + 674,378
		3. 483
		       964
		       827
		   + 691

4.   705,312
   − 95,605
	5. 869,403
	   − 351,674
		6. 800,261
		   − 358,273

7.   58
   × 67
	8. 431
	   × 296
		9. 73,058
		   × 2007

10. $37\overline{)26{,}085}$	**11.** $402\overline{)127{,}434}$	**12.** $85\overline{)340{,}510}$

40

Quiz

Word problems with whole numbers

Name _____

Date _____

Solve each problem.

1. Jerry has a newsstand on a downtown corner. During one week his daily sales were 743, 956, 821, 543, 686, 915, and 842 papers. How many papers did he sell during the week?	**2.** Ann belongs to a bowling league. Her scores on six lines of bowling were 183, 252, 196, 142, 221, and 125. What was her total for the six lines?
3. Betty is reading a book that has 1247 pages in it. She has read 869 pages. How many pages are left?	**4.** The school band is collecting coupons that will save money on new uniforms. They have collected 8952 coupons and need a total of 15,000. How many are yet to be collected?
5. The city library subscribes to 125 magazines at an average cost of $23 a year for each. What is the yearly cost of these magazines?	**6.** Bill averages 14 km to the liter of gasoline on his new compact car. How many kilometers can he drive on 112 gallons?
7. A profit of $281,295 is to be divided equally among 47 stockholders. How much is each share?	**8.** James spends a total of $300 for lunches over a period of 75 days. What is the average amount he spends each day?

41

Solve each problem.

1. Paul's scores for five pinball machine games were 87,550; 52,120; 69,000; 142,640, and 121,100. What was the total of his five scores?	**2.** Sonja spent $53, $120, $184, $215 and $76 for clothes during the school year. What was the total of her expenditure for clothes for the year?
3. During a bicycle race, Carol rode 21,550 meters and Gina rode 27,445 meters. How much farther did Gina ride than Carol?	**4.** Barbara had $2641 in her checking account and decided to put $840 of it into her savings account. How much was left in the checking account after the transfer?
5. One hundred fifty people attended an awards banquet. Each paid $5 for a ticket. What was the total value of the 150 tickets?	**6.** A train travels an average of 72 km per hour over a certain track. How many kilometers will it travel in 62 hours?
7. A hiker walked 560 km in 35 days. How many kilometers did he average each day?	**8.** A truck was loaded with sacks of potatoes. The total mass of the 550 sacks in the load was 24,750 kilograms. How many kilograms of potatoes were in each bag?

Name _____

Date _____

Solve each problem.

1. Ms. Bailey took a week to drive from San Francisco to New York City. The daily mileage totals were 312, 348, 365, 300, 381, 320, and 337. What was the total number of miles she drove on the trip?	**2.** Joey earned the following amounts during the twelve months in a year: $158, $160, $182, $112, $125, $110, $205, $210, $120, $133, $150, and $203. What were his total earnings for the year?
3. The total surface area of the state of Oklahoma is 69,919 square miles. If 1137 square miles of this surface area is covered by water, how many square miles of land surface area does Oklahoma have?	**4.** The Peachtree Center Plaza Hotel in Atlanta, Georgia is 721 feet high. The World Trade Center in New York City is 1350 feet high. How many feet higher is the World Trade Center than the Peachtree Center Plaza Hotel?
5. Willie collected $27 from each of 15 players on the football team to pay for a skiing trip they planned. What was the total amount of money he collected?	**6.** A bookstore has 253 shelves, each holding 155 books. If the shelves are full, how many books are there?
7. Shurvonne drove her car 1938 miles on 51 gallons of gasoline. How many miles per gallon did she average?	**8.** Warren paid a total of $9792 for house payments in 12 equal monthly payments. How much was each payment?

Solve each problem.

1. On six tests during a semester, a mathematics student had the following points: 92, 86, 143, 135, 63, and 98. What was the total number of points earned on the six tests?	**2.** Alaska has a total surface area of 586,412 square miles, Texas has 267,338 square miles, California has 158,693 square miles, Montana has 147,138 square miles, and New Mexico has 121,666 square miles. What is the total surface area of these five states?
3. Gannett Peak at 13,804 feet is the highest point in the state of Wyoming. The Fourche River at 3100 feet is the lowest point in the state. What is the difference in these two altitudes?	**4.** Dale borrowed $85,500 and paid back $17,625. How much does he still owe on the loan?
5. Tom rode 32 miles on the commuter train for each of 240 days. What was the total number of miles he rode the train for these days?	**6.** A certain auto manufacturing plant produces 57 cars per day for each of the 365 days in a year. What is the total yearly auto production in this plant?
7. There are 265 textbooks for a science class. They cost a total of $2915. Each book costs the same amount. What is the cost of each book?	**8.** A motorcycle costs $2548. Lynne earns $26 each day, on the average. How many days must she work in order to pay for the cycle?

44

Name _____

Date _____

Write = or ≠ to make a true statement.

1. $\frac{3}{4}$ $\frac{30}{40}$	**2.** $\frac{35}{56}$ $\frac{15}{21}$	**3.** $\frac{38}{40}$ $\frac{21}{27}$

Solve for *x*.

4. $\frac{16}{30} = \frac{x}{150}$	**5.** $\frac{x}{14} = \frac{13}{182}$	**6.** $\frac{36}{x} = \frac{12}{7}$
7. $\frac{11}{24} = \frac{x}{96}$	**8.** $\frac{x}{90} = \frac{13}{15}$	**9.** $\frac{6}{19} = \frac{48}{x}$
10. $\frac{56}{x} = \frac{7}{23}$	**11.** $\frac{5}{7} = \frac{x}{49}$	**12.** $\frac{10}{19} = \frac{90}{x}$

45

Quiz
Proportions

Name _____

Date _____

Write = or ≠ to make a true statement.

1. $\dfrac{6}{9}$ $\dfrac{14}{20}$	2. $\dfrac{28}{32}$ $\dfrac{70}{75}$	3. $\dfrac{18}{21}$ $\dfrac{72}{84}$

Solve for x.

4. $\dfrac{36}{60} = \dfrac{12}{x}$	5. $\dfrac{x}{5} = \dfrac{16}{20}$	6. $\dfrac{49}{42} = \dfrac{x}{6}$
7. $\dfrac{88}{99} = \dfrac{8}{x}$	8. $\dfrac{5}{x} = \dfrac{35}{49}$	9. $\dfrac{27}{36} = \dfrac{x}{4}$
10. $\dfrac{60}{66} = \dfrac{10}{x}$	11. $\dfrac{x}{7} = \dfrac{40}{56}$	12. $\dfrac{7}{x} = \dfrac{91}{156}$

Name _____

Date _____

Write = or ≠ to make a true statement.

1. $\dfrac{10}{12}$ $\dfrac{35}{40}$	2. $\dfrac{27}{33}$ $\dfrac{72}{88}$	3. $\dfrac{45}{54}$ $\dfrac{30}{36}$

Solve for x.

4. $\dfrac{84}{91} = \dfrac{x}{13}$	5. $\dfrac{12}{36} = \dfrac{x}{72}$	6. $\dfrac{4}{25} = \dfrac{16}{x}$
7. $\dfrac{x}{88} = \dfrac{3}{8}$	8. $\dfrac{9}{x} = \dfrac{81}{108}$	9. $\dfrac{x}{9} = \dfrac{24}{54}$
10. $\dfrac{14}{12} = \dfrac{7}{x}$	11. $\dfrac{x}{5} = \dfrac{45}{25}$	12. $\dfrac{55}{30} = \dfrac{11}{x}$

Quiz
Proportions

Name _____

Date _____

Write = or ≠ to make a true statement.

1. $\frac{42}{54}$ $\frac{56}{70}$	**2.** $\frac{30}{34}$ $\frac{60}{88}$	**3.** $\frac{56}{76}$ $\frac{42}{57}$

Solve for *x*.

4. $\frac{48}{75} = \frac{x}{125}$	**5.** $\frac{x}{8} = \frac{63}{72}$	**6.** $\frac{192}{84} = \frac{x}{7}$
7. $\frac{1}{x} = \frac{16}{64}$	**8.** $\frac{55}{121} = \frac{5}{x}$	**9.** $\frac{x}{13} = \frac{56}{91}$
10. $\frac{72}{117} = \frac{x}{13}$	**11.** $\frac{48}{112} = \frac{3}{x}$	**12.** $\frac{5}{x} = \frac{160}{256}$

48

Name _____

Date _____

Find each sum. Reduce each answer to lowest terms.

1. $\dfrac{2}{3}$ $+ \dfrac{5}{6}$	2. $\dfrac{3}{4}$ $+ \dfrac{3}{8}$	3. $\dfrac{4}{5}$ $+ \dfrac{7}{10}$
4. $\dfrac{2}{7}$ $+ \dfrac{5}{14}$	5. $\dfrac{1}{3}$ $+ \dfrac{3}{4}$	6. $\dfrac{1}{4}$ $+ \dfrac{4}{5}$
7. $\dfrac{2}{5}$ $+ \dfrac{1}{6}$	8. $\dfrac{2}{3}$ $+ \dfrac{3}{8}$	9. $\dfrac{5}{6}$ $+ \dfrac{4}{9}$
10. $\dfrac{3}{4}$ $+ \dfrac{5}{6}$	11. $\dfrac{5}{6}$ $+ \dfrac{3}{10}$	12. $\dfrac{3}{10}$ $+ \dfrac{7}{15}$

Quiz

Addition of fractions

Name _____

Date _____

Find each sum. Reduce each answer to lowest terms.

1. $\dfrac{2}{7}$ $+\ \dfrac{5}{14}$	2. $\dfrac{1}{5}$ $+\ \dfrac{9}{10}$	3. $\dfrac{1}{4}$ $+\ \dfrac{7}{8}$
4. $\dfrac{1}{6}$ $+\ \dfrac{2}{3}$	5. $\dfrac{1}{3}$ $+\ \dfrac{4}{7}$	6. $\dfrac{4}{7}$ $+\ \dfrac{2}{7}$
7. $\dfrac{3}{5}$ $+\ \dfrac{5}{6}$	8. $\dfrac{1}{4}$ $+\ \dfrac{3}{5}$	9. $\dfrac{2}{3}$ $+\ \dfrac{1}{4}$
10. $\dfrac{1}{4}$ $+\ \dfrac{7}{10}$	11. $\dfrac{1}{3}$ $+\ \dfrac{11}{15}$	12. $\dfrac{3}{10}$ $+\ \dfrac{8}{15}$

Quiz

Addition of fractions

Name _____

Date _____

Find each sum. Reduce each answer to lowest terms.

1. $\dfrac{1}{4}$ $+\dfrac{2}{3}$	2. $\dfrac{3}{4}$ $+\dfrac{1}{5}$	3. $\dfrac{2}{5}$ $+\dfrac{5}{6}$
4. $\dfrac{2}{5}$ $+\dfrac{3}{7}$	5. $\dfrac{1}{3}$ $+\dfrac{2}{7}$	6. $\dfrac{5}{7}$ $+\dfrac{3}{14}$
7. $\dfrac{2}{5}$ $+\dfrac{9}{10}$	8. $\dfrac{3}{4}$ $+\dfrac{1}{8}$	9. $\dfrac{1}{3}$ $+\dfrac{5}{6}$
10. $\dfrac{3}{4}$ $+\dfrac{7}{10}$	11. $\dfrac{1}{6}$ $+\dfrac{13}{15}$	12. $\dfrac{9}{10}$ $+\dfrac{11}{15}$

Find each sum. Reduce each answer to lowest terms.

1. $\begin{array}{r}\frac{2}{3}\\+\ \frac{4}{7}\\\hline\end{array}$	**2.** $\begin{array}{r}\frac{3}{5}\\+\ \frac{4}{7}\\\hline\end{array}$	**3.** $\begin{array}{r}\frac{4}{5}\\+\ \frac{1}{6}\\\hline\end{array}$
4. $\begin{array}{r}\frac{3}{4}\\+\ \frac{1}{5}\\\hline\end{array}$	**5.** $\begin{array}{r}\frac{1}{3}\\+\ \frac{1}{4}\\\hline\end{array}$	**6.** $\begin{array}{r}\frac{1}{3}\\+\ \frac{5}{6}\\\hline\end{array}$
7. $\begin{array}{r}\frac{3}{4}\\+\ \frac{7}{8}\\\hline\end{array}$	**8.** $\begin{array}{r}\frac{2}{5}\\+\ \frac{3}{10}\\\hline\end{array}$	**9.** $\begin{array}{r}\frac{5}{7}\\+\ \frac{3}{14}\\\hline\end{array}$
10. $\begin{array}{r}\frac{1}{4}\\+\ \frac{7}{10}\\\hline\end{array}$	**11.** $\begin{array}{r}\frac{1}{10}\\+\ \frac{4}{15}\\\hline\end{array}$	**12.** $\begin{array}{r}\frac{5}{6}\\+\ \frac{3}{10}\\\hline\end{array}$

Quiz

Subtraction of fractions

Name _____

Date _____

Find each difference. Reduce each answer to lowest terms.

1. $\dfrac{7}{8}$ $-\dfrac{1}{4}$	**2.** $\dfrac{2}{3}$ $-\dfrac{1}{2}$	**3.** $\dfrac{4}{5}$ $-\dfrac{2}{3}$
4. $\dfrac{5}{6}$ $-\dfrac{1}{8}$	**5.** $\dfrac{5}{8}$ $-\dfrac{5}{12}$	**6.** $\dfrac{4}{5}$ $-\dfrac{2}{3}$
7. $\dfrac{2}{3}$ $-\dfrac{3}{16}$	**8.** $\dfrac{4}{5}$ $-\dfrac{7}{12}$	**9.** $\dfrac{2}{3}$ $-\dfrac{3}{7}$
10. $\dfrac{5}{6}$ $-\dfrac{3}{8}$	**11.** $\dfrac{3}{4}$ $-\dfrac{2}{3}$	**12.** $\dfrac{5}{8}$ $-\dfrac{31}{64}$

Name _____

Date _____

Find each difference. Reduce each answer to lowest terms.

1. $\frac{4}{9}$ $-\frac{1}{3}$	**2.** $\frac{29}{45}$ $-\frac{7}{15}$	**3.** $\frac{26}{27}$ $-\frac{7}{9}$
4. $\frac{19}{20}$ $-\frac{4}{5}$	**5.** $\frac{5}{6}$ $-\frac{3}{8}$	**6.** $\frac{3}{4}$ $-\frac{1}{8}$
7. $\frac{2}{3}$ $-\frac{1}{6}$	**8.** $\frac{2}{3}$ $-\frac{1}{9}$	**9.** $\frac{5}{6}$ $-\frac{5}{9}$
10. $\frac{5}{6}$ $-\frac{1}{10}$	**11.** $\frac{7}{8}$ $-\frac{5}{12}$	**12.** $\frac{5}{7}$ $-\frac{1}{4}$

54

Name _____

Date _____

Find each difference. Reduce each answer to lowest terms.

1. $\begin{array}{r} \frac{5}{8} \\ -\ \frac{1}{4} \\ \hline \end{array}$	2. $\begin{array}{r} \frac{3}{4} \\ -\ \frac{1}{3} \\ \hline \end{array}$	3. $\begin{array}{r} \frac{5}{8} \\ -\ \frac{3}{5} \\ \hline \end{array}$
4. $\begin{array}{r} \frac{5}{6} \\ -\ \frac{3}{8} \\ \hline \end{array}$	5. $\begin{array}{r} \frac{7}{8} \\ -\ \frac{7}{12} \\ \hline \end{array}$	6. $\begin{array}{r} \frac{4}{5} \\ -\ \frac{1}{4} \\ \hline \end{array}$
7. $\begin{array}{r} \frac{2}{3} \\ -\ \frac{5}{16} \\ \hline \end{array}$	8. $\begin{array}{r} \frac{4}{5} \\ -\ \frac{5}{12} \\ \hline \end{array}$	9. $\begin{array}{r} \frac{2}{3} \\ -\ \frac{3}{7} \\ \hline \end{array}$
10. $\begin{array}{r} \frac{5}{6} \\ -\ \frac{5}{8} \\ \hline \end{array}$	11. $\begin{array}{r} \frac{5}{7} \\ -\ \frac{2}{5} \\ \hline \end{array}$	12. $\begin{array}{r} \frac{7}{12} \\ -\ \frac{1}{4} \\ \hline \end{array}$

Find each difference. Reduce each answer to lowest terms.

1. $\frac{17}{64}$ $-\frac{1}{8}$	2. $\frac{7}{8}$ $-\frac{1}{6}$	3. $\frac{11}{12}$ $-\frac{1}{8}$
4. $\frac{13}{14}$ $-\frac{1}{10}$	5. $\frac{15}{16}$ $-\frac{1}{6}$	6. $\frac{7}{12}$ $-\frac{1}{4}$
7. $\frac{6}{7}$ $-\frac{2}{21}$	8. $\frac{5}{6}$ $-\frac{1}{5}$	9. $\frac{1}{4}$ $-\frac{1}{14}$
10. $\frac{4}{15}$ $-\frac{1}{9}$	11. $\frac{73}{75}$ $-\frac{4}{15}$	12. $\frac{3}{10}$ $-\frac{2}{15}$

Quiz

Multiplication of fractions

Name _____

Date _____

Find each product. Reduce each answer to lowest terms.

1. $\frac{2}{15} \times \frac{11}{10} = ?$	**2.** $\frac{5}{8} \times \frac{48}{55} = ?$	**3.** Multiply $\frac{6}{13}$ by $\frac{52}{96}$.
4. Multiply $\frac{55}{70}$ by $\frac{7}{11}$.	**5.** $\frac{200}{500} \times \frac{45}{62} = ?$	**6.** $\begin{array}{r} \frac{2}{5} \\ \times \frac{3}{7} \\ \hline \end{array}$
7. Find the product of $\frac{33}{170}$ and $\frac{173}{55}$.	**8.** $\begin{array}{r} \frac{5}{27} \\ \times \frac{10}{27} \\ \hline \end{array}$	**9.** Multiply $\frac{7}{8}$, $\frac{2}{21}$, and $\frac{6}{15}$.
10. $11 \times \frac{7}{9} = ?$	**11.** Find the product of 13 and $\frac{5}{338}$.	**12.** $\frac{9}{35} \times \frac{5}{6} \times \frac{42}{99} = ?$

Copyright © 1981 by Dale Seymour Publications.

57

Find each product. Reduce each answer to lowest terms.

1. $\frac{3}{16} \times \frac{1}{15} = ?$	**2.** $\frac{8}{35} \times \frac{5}{72} = ?$	**3.** Multiply $\frac{5}{16}$ by $\frac{64}{125}$.
4. Multiply $\frac{77}{90}$ by $\frac{10}{7}$	**5.** $\begin{array}{r} \frac{2}{3} \\ \times \frac{5}{7} \\ \hline \end{array}$	**6.** Find the product of $\frac{55}{203}$ and $\frac{203}{66}$.
7. $\begin{array}{r} \frac{3}{23} \\ \times \frac{2}{23} \\ \hline \end{array}$	**8.** $6 \times \frac{36}{45} = ?$	**9.** Multiply $\frac{2}{3}$, $\frac{3}{5}$, and $\frac{5}{18}$.
10. $18 \times \frac{5}{8} = ?$	**11.** Find the product of 7 and $\frac{11}{462}$.	**12.** $\frac{5}{7} \times \frac{56}{90} \times \frac{6}{40} = ?$

58

Quiz

Multiplication of fractions

Find each product. Reduce each answer to lowest terms.

1. Find the product of $\frac{44}{56}$ and $\frac{28}{55}$.	2. $\frac{108}{132} \times \frac{11}{12} = ?$	3. Multiply $\frac{14}{26}$ by $\frac{13}{42}$.
4. $\frac{13}{49}$ $\times \frac{7}{39}$	5. $\frac{14}{26} \times \frac{13}{15} \times \frac{49}{56} = ?$	6. Find the product of $\frac{106}{136}$ and $\frac{15}{20}$.
7. $\frac{5}{11}$ $\times \frac{6}{31}$	8. $15 \times \frac{13}{45} = ?$	9. Multiply $\frac{58}{64}$ by $\frac{8}{29}$.
10. $20 \times \frac{2}{5} = ?$	11. Find the product of $\frac{18}{21}$ and $\frac{21}{9}$	12. $\frac{18}{20} \times \frac{56}{20} \times \frac{8}{9} = ?$

59

Name _____

Date _____

Find each product. Reduce each answer to lowest terms.

1. $\frac{3}{14} \times \frac{5}{6} \times \frac{7}{15} = ?$	**2.** $\frac{3}{4} \times \frac{11}{39} \times \frac{8}{77} = ?$	**3.** $\frac{16}{25} \times \frac{3}{8} \times \frac{9}{28} = ?$
4. $\frac{15}{32} \times \frac{8}{25} \times \frac{5}{22} = ?$	**5.** $\frac{6}{13} \times \frac{26}{39} \times \frac{15}{42} = ?$	**6.** $\frac{16}{35} \times \frac{14}{45} \times \frac{25}{36} = ?$
7. $\frac{34}{57} \times \frac{49}{51} \times \frac{38}{63} = ?$	**8.** $\frac{32}{75} \times \frac{45}{10} \times \frac{50}{27} = ?$	**9.** $\frac{12}{35} \times \frac{13}{27} \times \frac{14}{39} = ?$
10. $\frac{2}{3} \times 15 = ?$	**11.** $44 \times \frac{13}{11} = ?$	**12.** Multiply $\frac{18}{53}$ by $\frac{106}{16}$.

Quiz

Division of fractions

Name _____

Date _____

Find each quotient. Reduce each answer to lowest terms.

1. $\frac{12}{15} \div \frac{9}{45} = ?$	**2.** $\frac{\frac{22}{32}}{\frac{6}{8}} = ?$	**3.** Divide 9 by $\frac{3}{5}$.
4. Divide $\frac{8}{21}$ by 8.	**5.** $\frac{36}{48} \div \frac{3}{4} = ?$	**6.** $\frac{\frac{7}{25}}{\frac{21}{50}} = ?$
7. $\frac{3}{7} \div \frac{2}{5} = ?$	**8.** Divide $\frac{49}{60}$ by $\frac{7}{15}$.	**9.** $\frac{45}{52} \div 23 = ?$
10. Divide $\frac{51}{3}$ by 17.	**11.** $\frac{32}{75} \div \frac{8}{150} = ?$	**12.** $28 \div \frac{7}{8} = ?$

Division of fractions

Find each quotient. Reduce each answer to lowest terms.

1. $\frac{3}{8} \div \frac{1}{2} = ?$	**2.** Divide $\frac{3}{50}$ by $\frac{7}{10}$.	**3.** $\dfrac{\frac{5}{6}}{\frac{5}{42}} = ?$
4. Divide $\frac{9}{24}$ by $\frac{3}{8}$.	**5.** $\dfrac{\frac{25}{39}}{\frac{15}{13}} = ?$	**6.** $\frac{20}{700} \div \frac{5}{7} = ?$
7. $\dfrac{\frac{5}{6}}{\frac{25}{54}} = ?$	**8.** Divide $\frac{1}{4}$ by 7.	**9.** $\frac{16}{173} \div \frac{20}{173} = ?$
10. Divide $\frac{7}{8}$ by 2.	**11.** $\frac{1}{7} \div \frac{1}{2} = ?$	**12.** $\dfrac{\frac{30}{41}}{\frac{5}{6}} = ?$

Quiz

Division of fractions

Name _____

Date _____

Find each quotient. Reduce each answer to lowest terms.

1. $\frac{5}{9} \div \frac{1}{3} = ?$	**2.** Divide $\frac{11}{30}$ by $\frac{33}{20}$.	**3.** $\dfrac{\frac{7}{8}}{\frac{7}{4}} = ?$
4. Divide $\frac{16}{63}$ by $\frac{44}{56}$.	**5.** $\dfrac{\frac{15}{36}}{\frac{55}{42}} = ?$	**6.** $\frac{40}{300} \div \frac{48}{27} = ?$
7. $\dfrac{\frac{8}{9}}{\frac{18}{15}} = ?$	**8.** Divide $\frac{1}{3}$ by 8.	**9.** $\frac{18}{199} \div \frac{15}{199} = ?$
10. Divide $\frac{9}{8}$ by 3.	**11.** $\frac{1}{2} \div \frac{1}{7} = ?$	**12.** $\dfrac{\frac{28}{51}}{\frac{7}{3}} = ?$

Quiz

Division of fractions

Name _____

Date _____

Find each quotient. Reduce each answer to lowest terms.

1. $\frac{3}{5} \div \frac{9}{10} = ?$	**2.** $\frac{5}{6} \div \frac{7}{12} = ?$	**3.** $\dfrac{\frac{3}{4}}{6} = ?$
4. Divide $\frac{3}{4}$ by $\frac{3}{8}$.	**5.** $5 \div \frac{15}{16} = ?$	**6.** $\dfrac{\frac{2}{3}}{\frac{5}{8}} = ?$
7. $\dfrac{\frac{7}{8}}{\frac{5}{6}} = ?$	**8.** Divide 4 by $\frac{2}{5}$.	**9.** $\frac{9}{16} \div \frac{2}{5} = ?$
10. Divide $\frac{1}{4}$ by $\frac{3}{4}$.	**11.** $\dfrac{7}{\frac{1}{8}} = ?$	**12.** $6 \div \frac{4}{5} = ?$

Find each answer. Reduce each answer to lowest terms.

1. $\begin{array}{r} \frac{5}{13} \\ + \frac{7}{39} \\ \hline \end{array}$	2. $\begin{array}{r} \frac{1}{2} \\ \frac{2}{3} \\ + \frac{13}{14} \\ \hline \end{array}$	3. $\begin{array}{r} \frac{3}{16} \\ + \frac{17}{20} \\ \hline \end{array}$
4. $\begin{array}{r} \frac{3}{4} \\ - \frac{5}{12} \\ \hline \end{array}$	5. Find the difference between $\frac{5}{8}$ and $\frac{1}{4}$.	6. Subtract $\frac{7}{10}$ from $\frac{13}{16}$.
7. $\frac{3}{14} \times \frac{5}{6} \times \frac{7}{15} = ?$	8. Find the product of $\frac{3}{4}$, $\frac{11}{39}$, and $\frac{8}{77}$.	9. $\frac{16}{15} \times \frac{3}{8} \times \frac{9}{28} = ?$
10. $\frac{3}{7} \div \frac{15}{14} = ?$	11. Divide $\frac{64}{60}$ by $\frac{6}{8}$.	12. $\dfrac{\frac{8}{21}}{\frac{3}{10}} = ?$

65

Name _____

Date _____

Find each answer. Reduce each answer to lowest terms.

1. Find the sum of $\frac{5}{17}$ and $\frac{45}{51}$.	2. $\begin{array}{r} \frac{2}{15} \\ \frac{3}{4} \\ + \frac{7}{12} \\ \hline \end{array}$	3. $\frac{3}{16} + \frac{17}{20} = ?$
4. $\frac{4}{5} - \frac{3}{4} = ?$	5. Find the difference between $\frac{5}{6}$ and $\frac{3}{8}$.	6. Subtract $\frac{21}{32}$ from $\frac{15}{16}$.
7. $\frac{15}{32} \times \frac{8}{25} \times \frac{5}{22} = ?$	8. Find the product of $\frac{6}{13}$, $\frac{26}{45}$, and $\frac{15}{42}$.	9. $\frac{16}{35} \times \frac{14}{45} \times \frac{25}{36} = ?$
10. $\frac{13}{48} \div \frac{39}{136} = ?$	11. Divide $\frac{32}{45}$ by $\frac{8}{5}$.	12. $\dfrac{\frac{10}{51}}{\frac{25}{34}} = ?$

Find each answer. Reduce each answer to lowest terms.

1. $\frac{3}{5} + \frac{7}{19} = ?$	**2.** $\begin{array}{r} \frac{5}{6} \\ \frac{3}{8} \\ + \frac{7}{16} \\ \hline \end{array}$	**3.** Add $\frac{7}{16}$ and $\frac{41}{48}$.
4. $\frac{11}{16} - \frac{9}{20} = ?$	**5.** Find the difference between $\frac{7}{8}$ and $\frac{2}{3}$.	**6.** Subtract $\frac{7}{16}$ from $\frac{2}{3}$.
7. $\frac{34}{57} \times \frac{49}{51} \times \frac{38}{63} = ?$	**8.** Find the product of $\frac{12}{35}$, $\frac{13}{27}$, and $\frac{14}{39}$.	**9.** $\frac{32}{75} \times \frac{45}{10} \times \frac{50}{27} = ?$
10. $\frac{100}{200} \div \frac{7}{8} = ?$	**11.** Divide 8 by $\frac{7}{10}$.	**12.** $\dfrac{\frac{7}{8}}{\frac{3}{4}} = ?$

Quiz

Review of fractions

Name _____

Date _____

Find each answer. Reduce each answer to lowest terms.

1. Find the sum of $\frac{20}{63}$ and $\frac{9}{49}$.	**2.** $\begin{array}{r}\frac{2}{3}\\\frac{4}{17}\\+\ \frac{26}{51}\\\hline\end{array}$	**3.** Add $\frac{11}{20}$ and $\frac{3}{35}$.
4. $\begin{array}{r}\frac{3}{5}\\-\ \frac{7}{12}\\\hline\end{array}$	**5.** Find the difference between $\frac{5}{16}$ and $\frac{7}{8}$.	**6.** Subtract $\frac{3}{4}$ from $\frac{11}{12}$.
7. $\frac{6}{35} \times \frac{5}{16} \times \frac{28}{27} = ?$	**8.** Find the product of $\frac{14}{39}$, $\frac{13}{66}$, and $\frac{55}{56}$.	**9.** $\frac{9}{63} \times \frac{15}{45} \times \frac{42}{99} = ?$
10. $\frac{1}{8} \div \frac{1}{6} = ?$	**11.** Divide $\frac{36}{55}$ by 4.	**12.** $\dfrac{\frac{65}{72}}{\frac{5}{12}} = ?$

Quiz

Addition of mixed numbers

Name _____

Date _____

Find each sum.

1. $\quad 4\frac{3}{5}$ $+\ 9\frac{1}{6}$	**2.** Find the sum of $2\frac{3}{4}$ and $2\frac{1}{12}$.	**3.** $\quad 2\frac{9}{16}$ $+\ \quad\frac{23}{32}$
4. $\quad 7\frac{11}{12}$ $\quad 2\frac{3}{10}$ $+\ 6\,\frac{3}{5}$	**5.** $\quad 7\frac{5}{6}$ $+\ 1\frac{3}{4}$	**6.** $\quad 9\frac{5}{9}$ $+\ 4\frac{8}{9}$
7. $\quad 5\frac{13}{16}$ $+\ 6\,\frac{1}{2}$	**8.** $\quad 5\frac{9}{10}$ $+\ 1\,\frac{2}{5}$	**9.** $\ 9\frac{2}{3}+5\frac{5}{6}+1\frac{1}{4}=?$
10. $\quad 5\,\frac{2}{3}$ $+\ 2\frac{9}{10}$	**11.** $\quad 7\,\frac{1}{2}$ $\quad 2\frac{3}{10}$ $+\ 6\,\frac{3}{5}$	**12.** $\quad 4\,\frac{3}{7}$ $+\ 3\frac{11}{14}$

Name _____

Date _____

Find each sum.

1. $\quad 2\frac{1}{4}$ $+\ 3\frac{3}{8}$	**2.** $\quad 9\frac{11}{12} + 10\frac{4}{9} = ?$	**3.** Find the sum of $6\frac{3}{4}$, $2\frac{1}{8}$, and $9\frac{1}{2}$.
4. Add $8\frac{3}{4}$ to $9\frac{2}{7}$.	**5.** $\quad 8\frac{4}{9}$ $+\ 2\frac{5}{12}$	**6.** $\quad 7\frac{1}{5}$ $+\ 5\frac{3}{4}$
7. $\quad 9\frac{13}{16}$ $+\ 1\frac{1}{5}$	**8.** $\quad 10\frac{1}{17}$ $+\ 9\frac{2}{51}$	**9.** $\quad 8$ $\quad 2\frac{1}{3}$ $+\ 5\frac{3}{4}$
10. $\quad 6\frac{1}{2}$ $+\ 8\frac{2}{5}$	**11.** $\quad 3\frac{1}{5}$ $\quad \frac{2}{3}$ $+\ 6\frac{4}{15}$	**12.** $\quad 9\frac{3}{5}$ $+\ 3\frac{1}{10}$

Name _____

Date _____

Find each sum.

1. $4\frac{3}{10}$ $+ \ \ \frac{7}{8}$	**2.** $2\frac{1}{2}$ $3\frac{4}{5}$ $+ \ 1\frac{2}{3}$	**3.** $2\frac{1}{3}$ $4\frac{1}{6}$ $+ \ 5\frac{1}{8}$
4. $5\frac{13}{16}$ $+ \ 6\frac{1}{2}$	**5.** $11\frac{3}{10}$ $+ \ \ 3\frac{7}{8}$	**6.** $1\frac{5}{6}$ $+ \ 8\frac{11}{12}$
7. Add $10\frac{7}{12}$ and $18\frac{15}{16}$.	**8.** $3\frac{19}{32} + 1\frac{11}{16} + 5\frac{3}{4} = ?$	**9.** $13\frac{5}{12}$ $+ \ \ \ \frac{11}{12}$
10. $4\frac{3}{5}$ $+ \ 9\frac{1}{6}$	**11.** $23\frac{7}{10}$ $+ \ 18\frac{2}{3}$	**12.** $6\frac{7}{12}$ $+ \ 7\frac{2}{3}$

Find each sum.

1. $\quad 12\frac{7}{8}$ $+ \ \ 3\frac{5}{8}$ $\overline{}$	**2.** $\quad 6\frac{3}{8}$ $+ \ 2\frac{1}{4}$ $\overline{}$	**3.** Find the sum of $8\frac{1}{12}$ and $7\frac{9}{16}$.
4. Add $4\frac{1}{5}$ and $2\frac{7}{15}$.	**5.** $\quad 3\frac{2}{15}$ $+ \quad \frac{2}{3}$ $\overline{}$	**6.** $\quad 3\frac{7}{9} + 2\frac{1}{3} + 3\frac{5}{6} = ?$
7. $\quad 21\frac{5}{6}$ $+ \ \ 3\frac{11}{12}$ $\overline{}$	**8.** $\quad 15\frac{17}{20}$ $+ \ 12\frac{7}{8}$ $\overline{}$	**9.** $\quad 4\frac{7}{25} + 2\frac{3}{4} = ?$
10. Find the sum of $11\frac{17}{20}$ and $4\frac{3}{4}$.	**11.** $\quad 3\frac{3}{8}$ $+ \ 1\frac{5}{16}$ $\overline{}$	**12.** $\quad 7\frac{2}{3}$ $+ \ 4\frac{3}{5}$ $\overline{}$

Quiz
Subtraction of mixed numbers

Name _____

Date _____

Find each difference.

1. $9\frac{5}{8}$ $-\ 4\frac{1}{4}$	2. $35\frac{1}{4}$ $-\ 15$	3. $40\frac{3}{4} - 39\frac{1}{4} = ?$
4. $3\ \frac{1}{2}$ $-\ 1\frac{1}{4}$	5. $17\frac{13}{16}$ $-\ 9\frac{5}{8}$	6. $12\frac{5}{8}$ $-\ 9\frac{1}{16}$
7. Subtract $2\frac{1}{3}$ from $3\frac{3}{4}$.	8. $5\frac{5}{16}$ $-\ 2\frac{15}{16}$	9. $2\frac{3}{8} - \frac{5}{16} = ?$
10. Find the difference between $62\frac{1}{3}$ and $27\frac{1}{3}$.	11. $11\ \frac{7}{8}$ $-\ 3\frac{3}{10}$	12. How much greater than $4\frac{1}{3}$ is $7\frac{1}{2}$?

73

Name _____

Date _____

Find each difference.

1. $9\frac{3}{16}$ $-\ 2\frac{5}{6}$	**2.** $11\frac{5}{8}$ $-\ 4$	**3.** 9 $-\ 2\frac{11}{16}$
4. $8\frac{1}{2} - 4\frac{2}{3} = ?$	**5.** 6 $-\ \frac{7}{8}$	**6.** Subtract $1\frac{15}{16}$ from $4\frac{1}{4}$.
7. How much greater than $2\frac{1}{3}$ is $3\frac{3}{4}$?	**8.** $9\frac{3}{8}$ $-\ 3\frac{15}{32}$	**9.** $5\frac{7}{8} - 3\frac{1}{2} = ?$
10. $5\frac{2}{3}$ $-\ 2\frac{9}{10}$	**11.** $7\frac{2}{3}$ $-\ 4\frac{1}{4}$	**12.** $18\frac{7}{12}$ $-\ 10\frac{5}{12}$

Quiz

Subtraction of mixed numbers

Name _____

Date _____

Find each difference.

1. $3\frac{1}{2}$ $-\ 3\frac{1}{4}$	**2.** $11\frac{3}{5}$ $-\ \ 9\frac{1}{4}$	**3.** $22\frac{5}{8}$ $-\ 12\frac{1}{2}$
4. Subtract $4\frac{3}{4}$ from $12\frac{5}{8}$.	**5.** $25\frac{7}{9}$ $-\ 16\frac{7}{12}$	**6.** $17\frac{2}{3}$ $-\ 15\frac{3}{4}$
7. How much greater than $4\frac{3}{4}$ is $5\frac{1}{8}$?	**8.** $10\frac{9}{10}$ $-\ \ 7\frac{1}{4}$	**9.** $13\frac{3}{4}$ $-\ 11\frac{1}{3}$
10. $10\frac{1}{3} - 8\frac{3}{4} = ?$	**11.** $9\frac{1}{2}$ $-\ 6\frac{3}{4}$	**12.** $34\frac{3}{5}$ $-\ 29\frac{1}{2}$

Quiz

Subtraction of mixed numbers

Name _____

Date _____

Find each difference.

1. $32\frac{4}{5}$ $-\ 19\frac{2}{3}$	**2.** Find the difference between $62\frac{1}{6}$ and $27\frac{1}{3}$.	**3.** $19\frac{5}{16}$ $-\ 12\frac{1}{4}$
4. $15\frac{3}{8}$ $-\ 14\frac{4}{5}$	**5.** $34\frac{3}{5}$ $-\ 29\frac{1}{2}$	**6.** $15\frac{3}{16}$ $-\ 14\frac{7}{8}$
7. $5\frac{9}{10}$ $-\ 4\frac{5}{6}$	**8.** $12\frac{5}{8}$ $-\ 9\frac{1}{6}$	**9.** $17\frac{3}{4}$ $-\ 5\frac{7}{8}$
10. Subtract $1\frac{3}{4}$ from $21\frac{1}{2}$.	**11.** Find the difference between $6\frac{5}{8}$ and $4\frac{3}{4}$.	**12.** $8\frac{2}{3} - 5\frac{1}{2} = \ ?$

Name _____

Date _____

Find each product.

1. $4\frac{1}{3} \times 3\frac{1}{5} = ?$	**2.** $5\frac{3}{5} \times 3\frac{4}{7} = ?$	**3.** $2\frac{1}{7} \times 2\frac{4}{5} = ?$
4. $7\frac{7}{10} \times 2\frac{1}{12} = ?$	**5.** $5\frac{7}{8} \times 1\frac{3}{47} = ?$	**6.** $3\frac{1}{8} \times 18 = ?$
7. $15 \times 2\frac{1}{5} = ?$	**8.** $3\frac{1}{7} \times 2\frac{1}{2} = ?$	**9.** $3\frac{1}{3} \times 10\frac{1}{2} = ?$
10. $11\frac{2}{3} \times 1\frac{4}{5} = ?$	**11.** $9\frac{5}{6} \times 7\frac{3}{8} = ?$	**12.** $4\frac{1}{11} \times 8\frac{5}{9} = ?$

Multiplication of mixed numbers

Name _____

Date _____

Find each product.

1. $3\frac{1}{5} \times 2\frac{1}{4} = ?$	**2.** $7\frac{2}{3} \times 1\frac{1}{4} = ?$	**3.** $4\frac{1}{5} \times 4\frac{2}{7} = ?$
4. $5\frac{1}{3} \times 4\frac{1}{2} = ?$	**5.** $6\frac{2}{5} \times 6\frac{3}{7} = ?$	**6.** $8\frac{1}{3} \times 9\frac{4}{5} = ?$
7. $3\frac{5}{6} \times 2\frac{5}{8} = ?$	**8.** $9\frac{7}{9} \times 3\frac{3}{4} = ?$	**9.** $7\frac{1}{4} \times 3\frac{1}{5} = ?$
10. $3\frac{1}{5} \times 2\frac{1}{2} = ?$	**11.** $3\frac{1}{2} \times 2\frac{2}{7} = ?$	**12.** $1\frac{4}{5} \times \frac{5}{18} = ?$

Quiz

Multiplication of mixed numbers

Name _____

Date _____

Find each product.

1. $18 \times 3\frac{1}{8} = ?$	**2.** $7\frac{1}{5} \times \frac{5}{6} = ?$	**3.** $6\frac{5}{6} \times 3\frac{7}{8} = ?$
4. $5\frac{1}{7} \times 3\frac{1}{9} = ?$	**5.** $2\frac{5}{8} \times 1\frac{1}{63} = ?$	**6.** $3\frac{1}{7} \times 1\frac{10}{11} = ?$
7. $9\frac{4}{5} \times 3\frac{4}{7} = ?$	**8.** $4\frac{3}{8} \times 4\frac{4}{5} = ?$	**9.** $5\frac{3}{5} \times 10\frac{5}{7} = ?$
10. $10\frac{1}{2} \times 2\frac{1}{7} = ?$	**11.** $1\frac{7}{15} \times 6\frac{2}{3} = ?$	**12.** $4\frac{12}{13} \times 4\frac{7}{8} = ?$

Name _____

Date _____

Find each product.

1. $5\frac{3}{5} \times 1\frac{13}{21} = ?$	**2.** $5\frac{1}{5} \times 12\frac{1}{2} = ?$	**3.** $2\frac{4}{5} \times 5\frac{5}{7} = ?$
4. $7\frac{1}{2} \times 2\frac{2}{5} = ?$	**5.** $1\frac{1}{3} \times 4\frac{1}{2} = ?$	**6.** $5\frac{5}{7} \times 2\frac{1}{10} = ?$
7. $1\frac{1}{63} \times 2\frac{5}{8} = ?$	**8.** $9\frac{1}{3} \times 6\frac{3}{4} = ?$	**9.** $9\frac{3}{8} \times 11\frac{1}{9} = ?$
10. $3\frac{1}{3} \times 1\frac{1}{5} = ?$	**11.** $22\frac{2}{3} \times 2\frac{1}{4} = ?$	**12.** $3\frac{3}{5} \times 7\frac{1}{2} = ?$

Quiz

Division of mixed numbers

Name _____

Date _____

Find each quotient.

1. $1\frac{5}{7} \div 3\frac{1}{2} = ?$	**2.** $3\frac{1}{8} \div 1\frac{1}{4} = ?$	**3.** $4\frac{1}{3} \div 1\frac{2}{3} = ?$
4. $5\frac{3}{5} \div \frac{7}{25} = ?$	**5.** $2\frac{1}{7} \div 1\frac{11}{14} = ?$	**6.** $2\frac{1}{12} \div 4\frac{1}{2} = ?$
7. $7\frac{7}{10} \div 1\frac{1}{10} = ?$	**8.** $3\frac{1}{8} \div 2\frac{1}{2} = ?$	**9.** $2\frac{1}{5} \div 3\frac{2}{25} = ?$
10. $3\frac{1}{3} \div 1\frac{2}{3} = ?$	**11.** $\dfrac{6\frac{2}{3}}{1\frac{1}{9}} = ?$	**12.** $\dfrac{8\frac{2}{3}}{12\frac{5}{6}} = ?$

Name _____

Date _____

Find each quotient.

1. $2\frac{1}{3} \div 3\frac{1}{9} = ?$	**2.** $2\frac{4}{5} \div 4\frac{1}{5} = ?$	**3.** $3\frac{1}{3} \div 3\frac{8}{9} = ?$
4. $6\frac{5}{6} \div \frac{5}{6} = ?$	**5.** $2\frac{4}{7} \div 1\frac{2}{7} = ?$	**6.** $16\frac{2}{3} \div 4\frac{1}{6} = ?$
7. $8\frac{1}{3} \div 6 = ?$	**8.** $4\frac{1}{6} \div 1\frac{2}{3} = ?$	**9.** $21\frac{1}{3} \div 2\frac{2}{3} = ?$
10. $2\frac{1}{3} \div 3\frac{1}{8} = ?$	**11.** $\dfrac{3\frac{4}{5}}{1\frac{3}{7}} = ?$	**12.** $\dfrac{1\frac{2}{3}}{4\frac{1}{6}} = ?$

Find each quotient.

1. $2\frac{1}{7} \div 1\frac{11}{14} = ?$	**2.** $3\frac{1}{2} \div 2\frac{5}{8} = ?$	**3.** $1\frac{2}{3} \div 2\frac{5}{8} = ?$
4. $2\frac{1}{2} \div 1\frac{1}{4} = ?$	**5.** $3\frac{1}{9} \div 2\frac{2}{5} = ?$	**6.** $12\frac{5}{6} \div 8\frac{2}{3} = ?$
7. $1\frac{1}{9} \div 6\frac{2}{3} = ?$	**8.** $3\frac{1}{8} \div 3\frac{1}{8} = ?$	**9.** $7 \div 2\frac{1}{3} = ?$
10. $9\frac{3}{7} \div 25\frac{2}{3} = ?$	**11.** $\dfrac{2\frac{5}{8}}{1\frac{1}{2}} = ?$	**12.** $\dfrac{1\frac{7}{8}}{7\frac{1}{4}} = ?$

83

Quiz
Division of mixed numbers

Name _____

Date _____

Find each quotient.

1. $1\frac{1}{4} \div 7\frac{1}{2} = ?$	**2.** $8\frac{1}{3} \div 4\frac{1}{6} = ?$	**3.** $5\frac{1}{5} \div 1\frac{3}{10} = ?$
4. $9\frac{1}{3} \div 2\frac{2}{9} = ?$	**5.** $2\frac{1}{2} \div 1\frac{1}{6} = ?$	**6.** $3\frac{1}{7} \div 2\frac{5}{14} = ?$
7. $4\frac{1}{6} \div 8\frac{1}{3} = ?$	**8.** $1\frac{3}{10} \div 5\frac{1}{5} = ?$	**9.** $2\frac{1}{7} \div 3\frac{1}{9} = ?$
10. $5\frac{1}{7} \div 1\frac{1}{21} = ?$	**11.** $\dfrac{6\frac{3}{8}}{3\frac{1}{4}} = ?$	**12.** $\dfrac{9\frac{5}{8}}{2\frac{3}{4}} = ?$

Name _____

Date _____

Find each answer.

1. $\quad 2\frac{3}{4}$ $\underline{+\ 3\frac{5}{8}}$	**2.** $\quad 4\frac{11}{12}$ $\underline{+\ 2\frac{5}{12}}$	**3.** $8\frac{13}{16} + 2\frac{3}{4} + 5\frac{1}{2} = ?$
4. $\quad 6\frac{13}{16}$ $\underline{-\ 2\frac{5}{16}}$	**5.** $\quad 7$ $\underline{-\ 1\frac{5}{6}}$	**6.** How much larger than 2 is $8\frac{1}{2}$?
7. $24 \times 4\frac{5}{8} = ?$	**8.** Find the product of $3\frac{3}{4}$ and $7\frac{1}{5}$.	**9.** $2\frac{1}{2} \times 10 = ?$
10. $6\frac{2}{3} \div 5\frac{5}{6} = ?$	**11.** $45 \div 1\frac{7}{8} = ?$	**12.** $\quad \dfrac{12\frac{1}{4}}{4} = ?$

85

Quiz

Review of mixed numbers

Name _____

Date _____

Find each answer.

1. $\quad 24\frac{9}{10}$ $+\ 17\frac{5}{8}$ $\overline{\qquad}$	**2.** $\quad 4\frac{1}{3}$ $\quad 8\frac{3}{8}$ $+\ 2\frac{3}{4}$ $\overline{\qquad}$	**3.** $2\frac{5}{6} + 3\frac{1}{10} + 4\frac{1}{2} = ?$
4. $\quad 36\frac{2}{3}$ $-\ 17\frac{7}{8}$ $\overline{\qquad}$	**5.** $4 - \frac{9}{16} = ?$	**6.** Find the difference between $9\frac{1}{16}$ and $2\frac{3}{5}$.
7. $2\frac{5}{8} \times 2\frac{2}{5} = ?$	**8.** Find the product of $2\frac{7}{8}$ and $1\frac{3}{4}$.	**9.** $1\frac{3}{4} \times 18 = ?$
10. $9\frac{1}{3} \div 3\frac{1}{7} = ?$	**11.** $11\frac{1}{3} \div 2\frac{5}{6} = ?$	**12.** $\quad \dfrac{3\frac{15}{16}}{2\frac{5}{8}} = ?$

Quiz

Review of mixed numbers

Name _____

Date _____

Find each answer.

1. $32\frac{9}{16}$ $+\ 15\frac{7}{12}$	**2.** $18\frac{5}{8}$ $13\frac{11}{12}$ $+\ 42\frac{3}{16}$	**3.** $4\frac{3}{10} + 8\frac{5}{12} = ?$
4. $6\frac{1}{2} - \frac{2}{3} = ?$	**5.** Find the difference between $18\frac{5}{6}$ and $12\frac{15}{16}$.	**6.** 42 $-\ 17\frac{7}{20}$
7. Find the product of $2\frac{3}{4}$, $1\frac{1}{8}$, and $3\frac{5}{6}$.	**8.** $1\frac{9}{16} \times 4\frac{1}{3} = ?$	**9.** Multiply 7 by $3\frac{1}{4}$.
10. Divide $3\frac{3}{4}$ by $4\frac{2}{5}$.	**11.** $\dfrac{68}{3\frac{2}{5}} = ?$	**12.** $62\frac{1}{2} \div 100 = ?$

87

Name _____

Date _____

Find each answer.

1. $16\frac{1}{3}$ $+\ 3\frac{1}{9}$ _____	2. $24\frac{5}{16}$ $+\ \ 8\frac{1}{4}$ _____	3. $14\frac{5}{6}$ $2\frac{3}{4}$ $+\ \ 5\frac{7}{8}$ _____
4. $28\frac{4}{15}$ $-\ 15\frac{20}{21}$ _____	5. $8\frac{1}{3} - 2\frac{3}{4} = ?$	6. Find the difference between $16\frac{1}{8}$ and $7\frac{2}{3}$.
7. $3\frac{8}{9} \times 1\frac{2}{7} = ?$	8. $7\frac{1}{4} \times 2\frac{1}{10} = ?$	9. Find the product of $3\frac{1}{5}$ and $2\frac{1}{4}$.
10. $7\frac{7}{10} \div 1\frac{1}{10} = ?$	11. $\dfrac{3\frac{3}{4}}{4\frac{3}{8}} = ?$	12. Divide $7\frac{2}{9}$ by $4\frac{7}{12}$.

88

Name _____

Date _____

Solve each problem.

1. John needs three pieces of cloth measuring $5\frac{1}{2}$, $28\frac{1}{2}$, and $15\frac{3}{4}$ inches. What is the total number of inches of cloth?	**2.** Mary hiked $20\frac{1}{2}$ miles, $24\frac{1}{4}$ miles and $28\frac{3}{4}$ miles on three days. What is the total distance she hiked?
3. John is $69\frac{1}{2}$ inches tall. Bill is $71\frac{3}{4}$ inches tall. How much taller is Bill than John?	**4.** Rita hiked $7\frac{5}{6}$ miles. Nancy hiked $5\frac{7}{8}$ miles. How much farther did Rita hike than Nancy?
5. Ramon had $2\frac{1}{2}$ pounds of grapes. He gave his sister half of them. How many pounds did he have left?	**6.** A raisin nut cake recipe calls for $1\frac{1}{3}$ cups of raisins. The recipe is to be doubled. How many cups of raisins should be used?
7. How many one-thirds are there in $7\frac{1}{3}$?	**8.** A board $27\frac{1}{2}$ feet long is to be cut into 5 pieces. How long will each piece be?

89

Quiz

Word problems with mixed numbers

Name _____

Date _____

Solve each problem.

1. In a relay race Ann ran $45\frac{1}{4}$ yards, Jill ran $40\frac{1}{3}$ yards, and Dinah ran $42\frac{1}{16}$ yards. What was the total number of yards the girls ran?

2. John needs 3 pieces of lumber to complete a project. The pieces measure $5\frac{3}{4}$, $3\frac{1}{2}$, and $4\frac{1}{2}$ feet. What is the total number of feet needed?

3. Mike bought $3\frac{1}{2}$ pounds of fruit and $4\frac{7}{8}$ pounds of vegetables. How many more pounds of vegetables than fruit did he buy?

4. Bryan bought $2\frac{1}{2}$ pounds of cookies. His friends ate $1\frac{7}{8}$ pounds of them. How many pounds of cookies were left?

5. Grant lives $2\frac{1}{4}$ miles from school. His mother drove him $\frac{1}{3}$ of this distance. How far did she drive him?

6. A lake is $3\frac{9}{16}$ miles wide. How far is it to the middle of the lake from one bank?

7. How many one-fourths are there in $7\frac{5}{8}$?

8. A board $8\frac{2}{3}$ feet long is to be cut into 6 pieces. How long will each piece be?

90

Solve each problem.

1. Angie hiked $18\frac{1}{4}$, $20\frac{1}{2}$, and $22\frac{1}{8}$ miles in three days. What is the total distance she hiked?	**2.** Peter bought $5\frac{1}{2}$ pounds of cherries, $3\frac{1}{4}$ pounds of apples, and $4\frac{1}{8}$ pounds of oranges. How many pounds of fruit did he buy?
3. Janet is $66\frac{3}{4}$ inches tall. Carol is $64\frac{7}{8}$ inches tall. How much taller is Janet than Carol?	**4.** June jogged $2\frac{15}{16}$ miles. Tracy jogged $3\frac{1}{2}$ miles. How much farther did Tracy jog?
5. A moving van carried $3\frac{5}{7}$ tons of furniture to a new home and unloaded $\frac{1}{4}$ of it in 2 hours. How many tons of furniture was unloaded in 2 hours?	**6.** A recipe calls for $4\frac{1}{2}$ cups of flour. The recipe is to be tripled. How much flour should be used?
7. How many one-fifths are there in $6\frac{3}{10}$?	**8.** A length of piece goods $5\frac{1}{2}$ yards long is to be cut into 3 pieces. How long will each piece be?

91

Solve each problem.

1. Vera drove $53\frac{7}{8}$ miles, $24\frac{3}{4}$ miles, and $49\frac{1}{2}$ miles in three days. How many miles did she drive?	**2.** Three people in an elevator weigh $235\frac{1}{2}$ pounds, $197\frac{3}{4}$ pounds, and $142\frac{3}{16}$ pounds. What is their total weight? The capacity of the elevator is 1000 pounds. Is the elevator overloaded?
3. Pearl purchased $3\frac{1}{2}$ yards of poster paper. She used $2\frac{7}{8}$ yards of it. How many yards did she have left?	**4.** Gary bought $7\frac{1}{2}$ feet of lumber. He used $5\frac{7}{8}$ feet of it. How much lumber did he have left?
5. Janet lives $2\frac{5}{8}$ miles from school. After walking $\frac{1}{3}$ of this distance she stopped to rest. How far had she walked at this time?	**6.** A recipe for pecan pie calls for $1\frac{1}{2}$ cups of sugar. A pie $1\frac{1}{2}$ times as large is to be made. How much sugar will be needed?
7. How many portions of $8\frac{3}{4}$ ounces each can be made from a boneless roast weighing 28 pounds? (Remember, 1 pound = 16 ounces.)	**8.** A piece of cloth $7\frac{3}{4}$ yards long is to be cut into 5 pieces. How long will each piece be?

Find each answer.

1. Write in words: 3217	**2.** Write in words: 43.821
3. Write with numerals: seventy thousand, fifty-five	**4.** Write with numerals: Three hundred and one hundred twenty-two thousandths
5. Write the equivalent decimal: $\frac{1}{3}$	**6.** Write the equivalent decimal: $\frac{5}{8}$
7. Write the equivalent reduced fraction: 0.44	**8.** Write the equivalent reduced fraction: 9.865
9. Round to the hundreds place: 3752	**10.** Round to the hundredths place: 56.4391
11. Round to the thousands place: 63,247	**12.** Round to the tenths place: 434.176

Quiz
Place value and rounding

Name _____

Date _____

Find each answer.

1. Write in words: 4379	**2.** Write in words: 476.083
3. Write with numerals: eight hundred ninety-four thousand, twenty-six	**4.** Write with numerals: six hundred twenty-two and thirty-seven hundredths
5. Write the equivalent decimal: $\frac{3}{11}$	**6.** Write the equivalent decimal: $\frac{7}{8}$
7. Write the equivalent reduced fraction: 0.68	**8.** Write the equivalent reduced fraction: 7.762
9. Round to the hundreds place: 8647	**10.** Round to the hundredths place: 68.6423
11. Round to the thousands place: 890,164	**12.** Round to the tenths place: 11.3972

Name _____

Date _____

Find each answer.

1. Write in words: 59,647	**2.** Write in words: 8674.93
3. Write with numerals: ninety-seven thousand, sixty-six	**4.** Write with numerals: two hundred two and ninety-eight thousandths
5. Write the equivalent decimal: $\frac{5}{7}$	**6.** Write the equivalent decimal: $\frac{5}{6}$
7. Write the equivalent reduced fraction: 0.94	**8.** Write the equivalent reduced fraction: 5.765
9. Round to the thousands place: 54,894.22	**10.** Round to the tenths place: 543.842
11. Round to the hundreds place: 8033.4	**12.** Round to the ones place: 473.8425

95

Name _____

Date _____

Find each answer.

1. Write in words: 9864	**2.** Write in words: 574.807
3. Write with numerals: nine thousand, six hundred two and eight hundredths	**4.** Write with numerals: five hundred thousand, and five thousandths
5. Write the equivalent decimal: $\frac{8}{9}$	**6.** Write the equivalent decimal: $\frac{15}{16}$
7. Write the equivalent reduced fraction: 0.68	**8.** Write the equivalent reduced fraction: 4.762
9. Round to the tenths place: 98.437	**10.** Round to the tens place: 649.8734
11. Round to the ones place: 800.379	**12.** Round to the hundredths place: 89.4372

Quiz

Ordering and adding decimals

Find each answer.

1. Circle the greatest number.	**2.** Circle the least number.	**3.** Circle the number closest to 85.
72.3 5.14169	1.007 13.6	8.514 82.371
13.00007 6.21	5 12.62	185.0 96.7
8.345	81.345	285.397

Find each sum.

4. 6.007 8.21 +13.67	**5.** 42.37 0.83 0.046 +27	**6.** Find the sum of 6.07, 0.0082, 8.6, and 9.
7. 63.47 + 0.82 + 0.095 = ?	**8.** Add 7.63, 0.0307, 8.2, and 19.	**9.** 175.6 0.083 0.0054 + 93
10. Find the sum of 16.053 and 182.4491.	**11.** Find the sum of 62.83, 0.97, 0.08, and 300.	**12.** Add 0.007, 0.092, 13.956, 0.812, and 367.835.

97

Quiz
Ordering and adding decimals

Name _____

Date _____

Find each answer.

| 1. Circle the greatest number.

3.25   7.1499983

12.1   11.23976

46 | 2. Circle the least number.

53.004   12.376

2.10039   14.98

1.3989 | 3. Circle the number closest to 175.

17.503   95.175

163.9987   275.3

43.62 |

Find each sum.

4.   5.003
    6.94
+17.7096
	5. 38.03
	    0.98
	    0.016
	+12
		6. Find the sum of 4.07, 0.0059, 3.6, and 76.

7. 69.31 + 0.63 + 0.953 = ?	8. 5.83 + 0.0606 + 3.5 + 95 = ?	9. 137.55
		    0.046
		    0.0039
		+ 58

10. Find the sum of 12.703 and 174.4466.	11. 58.37 + 0.89 + 0.30 + 7 = ?	12. Add 0.006, 0.053, 14.006, 0.116, and 537.95.

98

Quiz

Ordering and adding decimals

Name _____

Date _____

Find each answer.

1. Circle the greatest number.	2. Circle the least number.	3. Circle the number closest to 150.
4.75 3.9	59.807 12.1	15.15 1500
7.14998 0.03	3.79566 14	150.15 215.15
12.4 6.999989	1.3874 7.6	157 1150.5

Find each sum.

4.   3.004
          7.83
     +12.169
	5. 39.04
	          0.98
	          0.016
	     +25
		6. Find the sum of 3.09, 0.0093, 5.9, and 34.

7. 49.52 + 0.68 + 0.68 = ?	8. 4.98 + 0.0405 + 5.8 = ?	9. 193.66
		          0.069
		          0.0027
		     + 87

10. Find the sum of 13.904 and 154.3386.	11. 73.85 + 0.93 + 0.06 = ?	12. Add 0.006, 0.068, 14.862, 0.113, and 342.981.

Quiz

Ordering and adding decimals

Name _____

Date _____

Find each answer.

1. Circle the greatest number.	2. Circle the least number.	3. Circle the number closest to 55.
55.7 3.54721 0.0012 142.95 68.814	58 0.614 0.00012 45.3 82.17	5.56821 58.3 36.9 155.2 505.5

Find each sum.

4.   8.621
      29.6
     513
 +   0.473
	5. Find the sum of 0.92, 9.2, and 92.	6. 3.678
		     29.45
		     0.812
		    503.4
		 + 2.57

7. 49 + 4.9 +
     49.4 + 494 = ?
	8. 4.83 + 0.376 +
	     0.42 + 95 = ?
		9. 0.034
		     2.05
		   200.7
		 + 0.34

10. Find the sum of ·
     57.302 and 136.09.
	11. 3.72 + 0.487 + 9 = ?	12. Add 35.92, 0.68,
		     0.006, 30, and 3.1402.

Name _____

Date _____

Find each difference.

1. 9573.28 − 784.93	**2.** 936.42 − 78.98 = ?	**3.** How much less than 198 is 0.073?

4. Find the difference between 795.3 and 39.7.	**5.** 27.89
	  − 0.0097
		6. 58.007
		  − 38.978

7. 3000 − 587.63 = ?	**8.** 167.08 − 13.098	**9.** How much greater than 83.75 is 1900?
10. 187.66 − 107.975	**11.** Find the difference between 15.96 and 7.038.	**12.** 3897.02 − 958.79 = ?

Quiz

Subtraction of decimals

Name _____

Date _____

Find each difference.

1. How much less than 46.032 is 1.00727?	**2.** $\quad$ 0.50903 $\\ \underline{-0.376212}$	**3.** Find the difference between 372.483 and 297.697.
4. $\quad$ 352.70004 $\\ \underline{-272.83009}$	**5.** How much greater than 6.4572 is 13?	**6.** $\quad$ 43.5012 $\\ \underline{-\ 22.83}$
7. $\quad$ 727.301 $\\ \underline{-452.326}$	**8.** 57.251 − 29.35721 = ?	**9.** How much less than 235 is 187.23?
10. $\quad$ 20.531 $\\ \underline{-19.4832}$	**11.** Find the difference between 51 and 18.5239.	**12.** 1000 − 847.2935 = ?

102

Name _____

Date _____

Find each difference.

1.   329.63
   −143.94
	2. Find the difference between 86.698 and 41.602.	**3.** 0.95317
		   −0.42632

4. How much greater than 603.704 is 704.321?	**5.** 36,514.2
	  − 4,217.163
		6. 8.4004
		   −6.8216

7. 65.426 − 36.7 = ?	**8.** 33.0408 −12.706	**9.** How much less than 72 is 36.438?
10. Find the difference between 234 and 0.456.	**11.** 2436.81 − 946.026 = ?	**12.** 26,058.315 −12,656.808

Quiz

Subtraction of decimals

Name _____

Date _____

Find each difference.

1. 8434.62 − 846.35	**2.** 419.62 − 38.64 = ?	**3.** How much less than 170 is 0.035?

4. Find the difference between 895.4 and 27.6.	**5.** 39.87
	  − 0.0092
		6. 48.007
		  −43.928

7. 2000 − 876.93 = ?	**8.** 148.06 − 17.085	**9.** How much greater than 79.83 is 1495?
10. Find the difference between 14.38 and 7.069.	**11.** 3487.02 − 876.89 = ?	**12.** 42,735.095 − 712.874

Quiz

Multiplication of decimals

Find each product.

1. 3.59 × 4.2	**2.** Find the product of 28.7 and 3.5.	**3.** 0.173 × 0.66
4. Find the product of 75 and 7.92.	**5.** $69.4 \times 0.073 = ?$	**6.** $8.75 \times 4.016 = ?$
7. Multiply 78 and 8.7.	**8.** Find the product of 5.82 and 0.60.	**9.** 90.73 × 0.49
10. $8.02 \times 44 = ?$	**11.** Multiply 0.48 and 0.35.	**12.** $5.866 \times 730 = ?$

Quiz

Multiplication of decimals

Name _____

Date _____

Find each product.

1.   2.37
      ×   4.3
	2. Find the product of
	37.6 and 4.2.
		3. 0.173
		      × 0.44

4. Find the product of 73 and 9.32.	**5.** $46.7 \times 0.083 = ?$	**6.** Multiply 7.92 and 2.016.

7.   7.9
      × 9.3
	8. Find the product of
	4.72 and 0.30.
		9. 12.62
		     × 0.48

10. $9.06 \times 33 = ?$	**11.** Multiply 0.47 and 0.85.	**12.** $4.976 \times 0.760 = ?$

Quiz

Multiplication of decimals

Name _____

Date _____

Find each product.

1. 5.36 × 4.2	**2.** Find the product of 18.2 and 0.76.	**3.** 0.436 × 0.312
4. Find the product of 745 and 2.8.	**5.** 0.643 × 2.51 = ?	**6.** Multiply 3.642 by 4.7.
7. 23.4 × 32	**8.** Find the product of 43.6 and 10.7.	**9.** 32.4 × 0.612
10. 63.5 × 17 = ?	**11.** Multiply 0.3527 by 0.6.	**12.** Find the product of 3.65 and 1000.

107

Multiplication of decimals

Name _____

Date _____

Find each product.

1.   6.32
      ×   2.7
	2. Find the product of
	 67.82 and 0.27.
		3. 49.37
		      × 3.09

4. Find the product of 92.8 and 101.2.	**5.** 873.1 × 0.033 = ?	**6.** Multiply 997.3 by 0.85.

7.   8.26
      × 72.7
	8. Find the product of
	 62.7 and 32.9.
		9. 7.53
		      × 12.9

10. 92.3 × 0.29 = ?	**11.** 0.7621 × 0.032	**12.** Find the product of 659 and 0.62.

Name _____

Date _____

Find each quotient.

1. $6\overline{)0.5412}$	**2.** Divide 8.1341 by 0.13.	**3.** $0.8\overline{)12.288}$
4. Write $\frac{1}{8}$ in decimal form.	**5.** $5\overline{)0.68735}$	**6.** $\dfrac{458.2}{31.6} = ?$
7. $0.034\overline{)0.29648}$	**8.** Divide 11 by 0.025.	**9.** Write $\frac{7}{16}$ in decimal form.
10. $5.372 \div 0.34 = ?$	**11.** $0.07\overline{)0.11578}$	**12.** Divide 0.020319 by 0.0013.

Name _____

Date _____

Find each quotient.

1. $7\overline{)0.4207}$	**2.** Divide 0.3696 by 0.16.	**3.** $0.7\overline{)4.5787}$
4. Write $\frac{3}{8}$ in decimal form.	**5.** $5\overline{)0.68395}$	**6.** $\dfrac{889.22}{34.6} = ?$
7. $0.043\overline{)2.81263}$	**8.** Divide 9 by 0.075.	**9.** Write $\frac{5}{16}$ as a decimal.
10. $4.0544 \div 0.32 = ?$	**11.** $0.08\overline{)0.013912}$	**12.** Divide 0.024962 by 0.0014.

Quiz

Division of decimals

Name _____

Date _____

Find each quotient.

1. $9\overline{)0.6309}$	**2.** Divide 5.135 by 0.13.	**3.** $0.7\overline{)5.558}$
4. Write $\frac{7}{8}$ in decimal form.	**5.** $5\overline{)0.38935}$	**6.** $\frac{352.08}{32.6} = ?$
7. $0.029\overline{)1.3485}$	**8.** Divide 12 by 0.075.	**9.** Write $\frac{9}{16}$ in decimal form.
10. $19.832 \div 0.37 = ?$	**11.** $0.08\overline{)0.06432}$	**12.** Divide 0.54250 by 0.0014.

Quiz

Division of decimals

Name _____

Date _____

Find each quotient.

1. $7\overline{)0.476}$	2. Divide 0.5684 by 0.014.	3. $0.3\overline{)3.0609}$
4. Write $\frac{5}{8}$ in decimal form.	5. $0.42\overline{)84.042}$	6. $\dfrac{100.302}{0.006} = ?$
7. $0.0015\overline{)0.3075}$	8. Divide 1.6 by 0.008.	9. Write $\frac{11}{16}$ in decimal form.
10. $273.012 \div 0.30 = ?$	11. $0.03\overline{)025.02}$	12. Divide 2 by 0.005.

112

Name _____

Date _____

Find each answer.

1. Add 6932.17 and 2734.66.	**2.** $\begin{array}{r} 8.9112 \\ 67.543 \\ 2.66 \\ +1077.5614 \\ \hline \end{array}$	**3.** Add 6.21, 27.3, and 867.223.
4. $\begin{array}{r} 1003.32 \\ -\ \ 627.401 \\ \hline \end{array}$	**5.** $\begin{array}{r} 891.28 \\ -\ \ 67.39 \\ \hline \end{array}$	**6.** Subtract 27.697 from 866.4.
7. $\begin{array}{r} 2.7741 \\ \times\ \ \ \ 2.34 \\ \hline \end{array}$	**8.** $\begin{array}{r} 983.664 \\ \times\ \ \ \ 3.001 \\ \hline \end{array}$	**9.** $\begin{array}{r} 967.55 \\ \times\ \ \ \ 0.22 \\ \hline \end{array}$
10. $7.9\overline{)75.445}$	**11.** $56.7\overline{)114.0237}$	**12.** $21.9\overline{)1997.28}$

Find each answer.

1. Add 27.2739 and 793.21.	**2.** 4.033 29.68 472.622 + 4.0773	**3.** Add 10.11, 87.3, and 100.76.
4. 84.6928 −61.9989	**5.** 467.22 − 11.85	**6.** Subtract 47.881 from 756.92.
7. 72.832 × 2.44	**8.** 29.8956 × 41.12	**9.** 97.21 × 0.66
10. 3.9)‾25.155‾	**11.** 72.9)‾219.5748‾	**12.** 21.3)‾1393.02‾

Name _____

Date _____

Find each answer.

1. Add 46.1085 and 3.279.	**2.** $\begin{array}{r} 8.512 \\ 64.11 \\ 2.567 \\ +804.72 \\ \hline \end{array}$	**3.** Add 4.32, 69.7, and 7077.21.
4. $\begin{array}{r} 742.862 \\ -\ \ 64.98 \\ \hline \end{array}$	**5.** $\begin{array}{r} 27.87 \\ -24.985 \\ \hline \end{array}$	**6.** Subtract 63.285 from 751.69.
7. $\begin{array}{r} 4.37215 \\ \times\ \ \ \ \ 2.13 \\ \hline \end{array}$	**8.** $\begin{array}{r} 67.326 \\ \times\ \ \ 800.5 \\ \hline \end{array}$	**9.** $\begin{array}{r} 947.06 \\ \times\ \ \ \ 0.88 \\ \hline \end{array}$
10. $3.1\overline{)22.072}$	**11.** $87.3\overline{)174.6873}$	**12.** $17.4\overline{)1325.88}$

Quiz

Review of decimals

Name _____

Date _____

Find each answer.

1. Add 59.6723 and 2.712.	2. $\begin{array}{r} 6.314 \\ 82.95 \\ 3.002 \\ +905.81 \\ \hline \end{array}$	3. Add 8.35, 72.8, and 1004.675.
4. $\begin{array}{r} 937.621 \\ -59.28 \\ \hline \end{array}$	5. $\begin{array}{r} 43.96 \\ -12.858 \\ \hline \end{array}$	6. Subtract 54.372 from 836.54.
7. $\begin{array}{r} 3.8214 \\ \times 3.25 \\ \hline \end{array}$	8. $\begin{array}{r} 85.427 \\ \times 700.5 \\ \hline \end{array}$	9. $\begin{array}{r} 827.6 \\ \times 0.92 \\ \hline \end{array}$
10. $2.6\overline{)21.19}$	11. $92.7\overline{)98.1693}$	12. $14.6\overline{)1214.72}$

Name _____

Date _____

Solve each problem.

1. The Teshara family spent the following amounts for food during a six week period: $100.61, $98.52, $85.00, $123.79, $116.86, and $95.48. How much did they spend for food during those six weeks?	**2.** Mrs. Swann owns a catering company that brought in $586.25, $1186.90, $1250.00, $1585.75, $1401.50 and $2504.80 for the six working days of one week. What was the total amount brought in by the company?
3. A reservoir holds 53,633,200 gallons of water. This is 536.332 gallons for each person in the town. What is the population of the town?	**4.** Doma earned $15,805.14 during a year. She paid $2516.43 in taxes. How much did she have left after taxes?
5. A farm yields 25.7 bushels of corn per acre. 462.81 acres of corn are harvested. What was the total number of bushels of corn produced?	**6.** A city received 48.24 inches of rain during a year. What was the average for each of the twelve months of the year?
7. A city vaccinated 2300 animals for rabies. It took 1.26 cm³ of vaccine for each animal. How much vaccine was used?	**8.** Mark allowed himself $3500 for a trip to England. When he returned, he still had $486.15. How much did he spend on the trip?

Name _____

Date _____

Solve each problem.

1. A water tank has a volume of 8979.74 cubic feet. The tank holds 1200.5 gallons. How many gallons are in one cubic foot of water?	**2.** Mr. Walker's interest-bearing checking account earned the following amounts over a five-month period: $89.16, $74.25, $101.60, $51.21, and $63.50. What was the total amount of interest earned during that period?
3. John uses 0.25 ounces of black powder to reload one round of ammunition for his rifle. If he reloads 525 rounds in one year, how much powder will he use?	**4.** The stock market dropped from 989.54 to 966.87. How much did the stock market drop?
5. Darrell can drive his car 756.5 miles on a tank of fuel. How far can he drive his car on 17.31 tanks of fuel?	**6.** Vera had $2314.26 in her bank account at the beginning of the month. By the end of the month she had $863.58. How much did she spend?
7. Joanna returned from a fishing trip with six fish that weighed 1.2 pounds, 0.8 pounds, 3.6 pounds, 2.2 pounds and 2.0 pounds. What was the total weight of the fish?	**8.** Lila ran 2245.275 yards in 264.15 seconds. How many yards per second did she average?

118

Solve each problem.

1. Jim spent $12.49 for a shirt, $16.50 for jeans, and $68.35 for a jacket. Find the total cost of these items.	**2.** Ingrid has a bicycle shop. She collects sales tax which she sends in every four months. For the first four months of the year she collected $452.73, $581.62, $385.41, and $481.05. How much did she collect?
3. Joe and Juan together sold $853.25 in raffle tickets for a fund raising project. Joe sold $385.79. What was the amount that Juan sold?	**4.** The area of Rhode Island is 1214 square miles. The population is about 900,000. To the nearest whole number, what is the average population per square mile?
5. Jose has a large ranch in Arizona. He has 2347 calves to vaccinate. Each calf requires 1.57 cm³ of vaccine. How much vaccine will be required?	**6.** Tina harvested an average of 48.2 bushels per acre of wheat from the 157.36 acres she planted. How many bushels of wheat did she harvest?
7. The distance by rail from Buffalo to New York is 436.32 miles. The distance from Buffalo to Chicago is 510.1 miles. How much farther is it to Chicago than to New York?	**8.** The area of Alaska is 585,412 square miles. The population is about 400,000. To the nearest hundredth, what is the average area per person?

Solve each problem.

1. Two money-raising events brought the senior class $626.15. The car wash earned $227.50. What did the senior play earn?	**2.** A class-action law suit was settled by paying a total of $4,995,000 to a group of 900,000 persons. How much money did each person receive if the money was equally divided?
3. Betty earned the following amounts laying brick: $512.60, $425.50, $726.12, $900, and $327.67. What was the total amount she earned?	**4.** Arthur had $325 and spent $180.65. How much did he have left?
5. Ginny earned $123.16 each day for 27.5 days. What was her total earnings?	**6.** A gasoline tank on a car holds 19.6 gallons. The car averages 28.6 miles per gallon. How far can it travel on one tank of gasoline?
7. Julie jogged 3.4 miles on Saturday, 1.12 miles on Sunday, 2.58 miles on Monday and 5.03 miles on Tuesday. What was the total distance she jogged on these days?	**8.** The total land area of California is 156,361 square miles. California has a population of 22,000,000. What is the average amount of land per person, to the nearest thousandth?

Name _____

Date _____

Find each answer.

1. 4 is what percent of 5?	**2.** What percent of 12 is 6?	**3.** 0.62 is what percent?
4. $\frac{0.4}{100}$ equals what percent?	**5.** $\frac{5}{8}$ is what percent?	**6.** Find 33% of 42.
7. Write 5.2% as a decimal.	**8.** 19 is 25% of what number?	**9.** Write 72% as a fraction in lowest terms.
10. Find $33\frac{1}{3}$% of 99.	**11.** Find 12% of 54.	**12.** What percent of the figure is shaded?

Name _____

Date _____

Find each answer.

1. Write $\frac{3.5}{100}$ as a percent.	**2.** Find 16% of 68.	**3.** 0.0031 equals what percent?
4. 15 is what percent of 20?	**5.** Write 84% as a fraction in lowest terms.	**6.** Find 9.2% of 16.
7. $\frac{7}{8}$ equals what percent?	**8.** 24 is what percent of 20?	**9.** Write $\frac{5.7}{10}$ as a percent.
10. 45 is 75% of what number?	**11.** 17.5 equals what percent?	**12.** What percent of the figure is shaded?

Name _____

Date _____

Find each answer.

1. Write $\frac{2}{5}$ as a percent.	**2.** Write 0.16% as a decimal.	**3.** 4 is what percent of 5?
4. Find 17% of 63.	**5.** Write $\frac{0.51}{100}$ as a percent.	**6.** Find 30% of 80.
7. 27 is 25% of what number?	**8.** 20 is what percent of 50?	**9.** Find $12\frac{1}{2}$% of 104.
10. 7 is what percent of 35?	**11.** $\frac{7.6}{10}$ equals what percent?	**12.** What percent of the figure is shaded?

Quiz

Percents

Name _____

Date _____

Find each answer.

1. $\frac{1}{4}$ equals what percent?	**2.** 0.29 equals what percent?	**3.** Write 43% as a decimal.
4. $\frac{30}{100}$ equals what percent?	**5.** 20 is what percent of 100?	**6.** 15 percent of 35 equals what?
7. Find 75% of 36.	**8.** 42 is $66\frac{2}{3}$% of what number?	**9.** 18 is what percent of 90?
10. Write $5\frac{7}{10}$ as a percent.	**11.** Find 12.3% of 52.	**12.** What percent of the figure is shaded?

124

Solve each problem.

1. Find 20% of 135.	**2.** 35.69 is 43% of what number?
3. 13.12 is what percent of 82?	**4.** The regular price of a suit is $99. The suit is on sale for $33\frac{1}{3}$% off. Find the sale price.
5. A typewriter costs $150. It is on sale for $105. Find the rate of discount.	**6.** Dara borrowed $3000. She was charged interest at 15% per year. Find the interest for one year.
7. The sale price of a pair of shoes is $21. This is 70% of the regular price. Find the regular price.	**8.** Joe paid $100 interest on money he borrowed for one year. The rate of interest was 10%. How much money did he borrow?
9. A bicycle is advertised for sale at a 20% discount. The regular price is $150. Find the sale price.	**10.** The cost of a house increased 12% in one year. The original cost was $50,000. Find the cost one year later.

125

Solve each problem.

1. Find 25% of 248.	**2.** 23.49 is 27% of what number?
3. 31.92 is what percent of 76?	**4.** The regular price of a suit is $124. The suit is on sale for $12\frac{1}{2}$% off. Find the sale price of the suit.
5. Tom borrowed $2500. He was charged interest at 12% per year. Find the amount of interest for one year.	**6.** A typewriter is regularly priced at $250. It is on sale for $200. Find the rate of discount.
7. The sale price of a pair of shoes is $30. This is 75% of the regular price. Find the regular price.	**8.** Carol paid $120 interest on money she borrowed for one year. The rate of interest was 8%. How much money did she borrow?
9. A bicycle is advertised for sale at a 25% discount. The regular price is $180. Find the sale price.	**10.** The cost of a house increased 13% in one year. The original cost was $75,000. Find the cost one year later.

126

Name _____

Date _____

Solve each problem.

1. Find $37\frac{1}{2}\%$ of 88.	**2.** 25.92 is 36% of what number?
3. 41.85 is what percent of 93?	**4.** The regular price of a suit is $164. The suit is on sale for 25% off. Find the sale price of the suit.
5. A typewriter is regularly priced at $260. It is on sale for $227.50. Find the rate of discount.	**6.** The sale price of a pair of shoes is $28. This is $66\frac{2}{3}\%$ of the regular price. Find the regular price.
7. Ted borrowed $3200. He was charged interest at the rate of 9% per year. Find the interest for one year.	**8.** Nina paid $110 interest on money she borrowed for one year. The rate of interest was 5%. How much money did she borrow?
9. A bicycle is advertised for sale at a $33\frac{1}{3}\%$ discount. The regular price is $162. Find the sale price.	**10.** The cost of a house increased $12\frac{1}{2}\%$ in one year. The original cost was $84,000. Find the cost one year later.

127

Name _____

Date _____

Solve each problem.

1. Find $66\frac{2}{3}$% of 96.	**2.** 58.71 is 57% of what number?
3. 13.77 is what percent of 27?	**4.** The regular price of a suit is $150. The suit is on sale for 25% off. Find the sale price of the suit.
5. A typewriter is regularly priced at $300. It is on sale for $200. Find the rate of discount.	**6.** Tony borrowed $4300. He was charged interest at the rate of 11% per year. Find the interest for one year.
7. The sale price of a pair of shoes is $35. This is $62\frac{1}{2}$% of the regular price. Find the regular price.	**8.** Jessie paid $140 interest on money she borrowed for one year. The rate of interest was 7%. How much money did she borrow?
9. A bicycle is advertised for sale at a $12\frac{1}{2}$% discount. The regular price is $150. Find the sale price.	**10.** The cost of a house increased 15% in one year. The original cost was $90,000. Find the cost one year later.

128

Quiz

Equivalent measures

Name _____

Date _____

Complete.

1. 45°C = _____°F	**2.** 14°F = _____°C	**3.** 90°C = _____°F
4. 4 hr = _____ min	**5.** 42 days = _____ wk	**6.** 5 yr = _____ mo
7. 216 in. = _____ ft	**8.** 237,600 ft = _____ mi	**9.** 15 yd = _____ in.
10. 4200 ft = _____ yd	**11.** 2 mi = _____ yd	**12.** 17 ft = _____ in.

Name _____

Date _____

Complete.

1. 20°C = _____°F	**2.** 113°F = _____°C	**3.** 80°C = _____°F
4. 7 yr = _____ mo	**5.** 408 hr = _____ days	**6.** 192 mo = _____ yr
7. 47 m = _____ cm	**8.** 26 km = _____ m	**9.** 301 mm = _____ cm
10. 32 m = _____ mm	**11.** 520 cm = _____ m	**12.** 17 km = _____ m

Name _____

Date _____

Complete.

1. 35°C = _____°F	**2.** 140°F = _____°C	**3.** 50°C = _____°F
4. 660 sec = _____ min	**5.** 5 hr = _____ min	**6.** 12 yr = _____ mo
7. 1872 in. = _____ yd	**8.** 3 mi = _____ ft	**9.** 412 yd = _____ ft
10. 42 ft = _____ yd	**11.** 47 yd = _____ ft	**12.** 3 mi = _____ yd

Quiz

Equivalent measures

Name _____

Date _____

Complete.

1. 60°C = _____°F	**2.** 122°F = _____°C	**3.** 149°F = _____°C
4. 60 wk = _____ mo	**5.** 13 mo = _____ wk	**6.** 180 mo = _____ yr
7. 47 km = _____ m	**8.** 6152 mm = _____ m	**9.** 83 cm = _____ km
10. 0.59 cm = _____ mm	**11.** 63.5 m = _____ km	**12.** 82 mm = _____ m

Quiz

Angle measurement

Name _____

Date _____

Use a protractor to measure each angle.

1. ∠A: _____

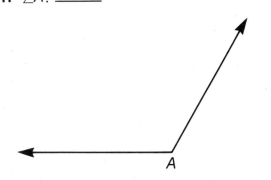

2. ∠B: _____

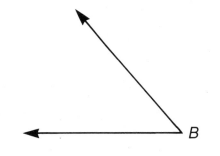

3. ∠C: _____
∠D: _____
∠E: _____

4. ∠F: _____
∠G: _____
∠H: _____

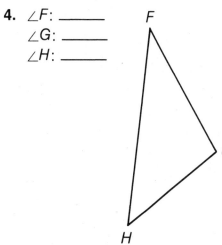

5. ∠J: _____
∠K: _____
∠L: _____
∠M: _____

6. ∠N: _____
∠O: _____
∠P: _____

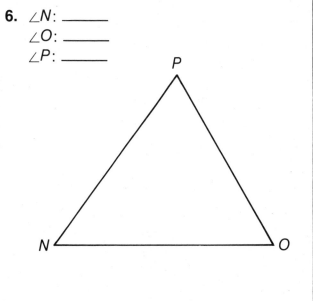

Use a protractor to measure each angle.

1. ∠A: _____

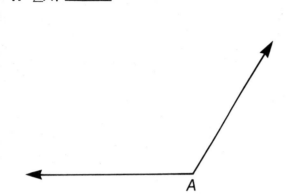

2. ∠B: _____

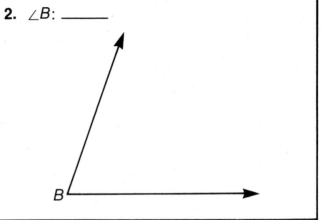

3. ∠C: _____
∠D: _____
∠E: _____

4. ∠F: _____
∠G: _____
∠H: _____

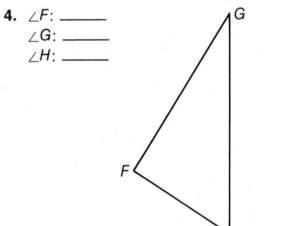

5. ∠J: _____
∠K: _____
∠L: _____

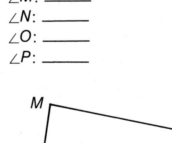

6. ∠M: _____
∠N: _____
∠O: _____
∠P: _____

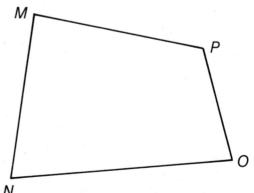

134

Name _____

Date _____

Use a protractor to measure each angle.

1. ∠A: _____

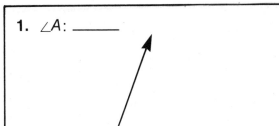

2. ∠B: _____

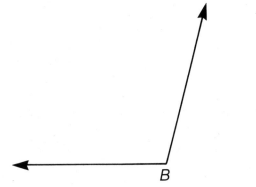

3. ∠C: _____
∠D: _____
∠E: _____

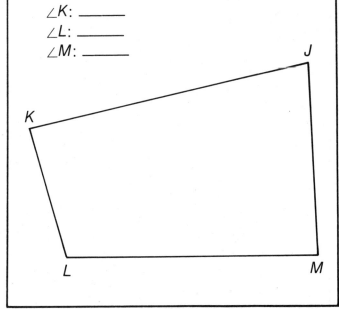

4. ∠F: _____
∠G: _____
∠H: _____

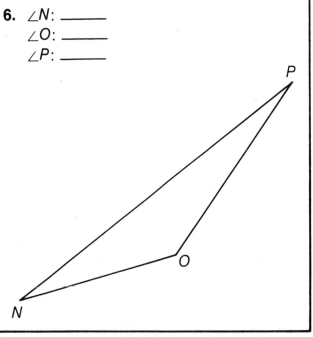

5. ∠J: _____
∠K: _____
∠L: _____
∠M: _____

6. ∠N: _____
∠O: _____
∠P: _____

135

Quiz

Angle measurement

Name _____

Date _____

Use a protractor to measure each angle.

1. ∠A: _____

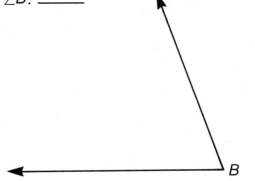

A

2. ∠B: _____

B

3. ∠C: _____
∠D: _____
∠E: _____

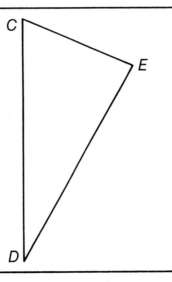

C

E

D

4. ∠F: _____
∠G: _____
∠H: _____

H

G

F

5. ∠J: _____
∠K: _____
∠L: _____

J

K   L

6. ∠M: _____
∠N: _____
∠O: _____
∠M: _____

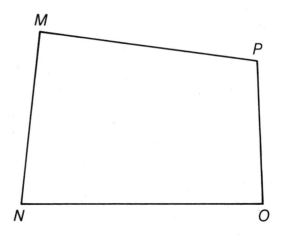

M

P

N   O

Find the area A and perimeter P of each rectangle. Be sure to use units in your answers.

$A = l \times w$
$P = 2l + 2w$

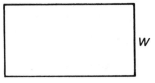

w

l

	l	w	Area	Perimeter
1.	$2\frac{1}{2}$ in.	$1\frac{1}{4}$ in.		
2.	2 yd	1 yd		
3.	$2\frac{1}{2}$ ft	2 ft		
4.	$3\frac{1}{2}$ in.	$3\frac{1}{2}$ in.		
5.	$2\frac{1}{4}$ mi	$1\frac{1}{4}$ mi		

137

Quiz

Area and perimeter of rectangles

Name _____

Date _____

Find the area A and perimeter P of each rectangle. Be sure to use units in your answers.

$A = l \times w$
$P = 2l + 2w$

	l	w	Area	Perimeter
1.	2.5 m	1.5 m		
2.	2.25 km	1 km		
3.	1.75 dm	1.75 dm		
4.	4.25 m	1.25 m		
5.	5.25 cm	1.5 cm		

Quiz

Area and perimeter of rectangles

Name _____

Date _____

Find the area A and perimeter P of each rectangle. Be sure to use units in your answers.

$A = l \times w$
$P = 2l + 2w$

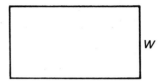
w

l

	l	w	Area	Perimeter
1.	$2\frac{1}{2}$ in.	$1\frac{1}{4}$ in.		
2.	$2\frac{3}{4}$ mi	2 mi		
3.	3 ft	$1\frac{1}{2}$ ft		
4.	$3\frac{1}{4}$ yd	$1\frac{1}{2}$ yd		
5.	4 in.	$\frac{3}{4}$ in.		

139

Quiz

Area and perimeter of rectangles

Name _____

Date _____

Find the area A and perimeter P of each rectangle. Be sure to use units in your answers.

$A = l \times w$
$P = 2l + 2w$

	l	w	Area	Perimeter
1.	2.5 km	1.75 km		
2.	2 dm	1.25 dm		
3.	3.75 m	2.25 m		
4.	2.5 km	1.4 km		
5.	4.25 cm	1 cm		

140

Name _____

Date _____

Measure the length of the sides and the altitude of each figure to the nearest quarter-inch. Find the area and perimeter of each. Be sure to write units in your answers.

Triangle

$A = \frac{1}{2} b \times h$

$P = a + b + c$

Parallelogram

$A = b \times h$

$P = 2a + 2b$

Trapezoid

$A = \frac{1}{2} h (b_1 + b_2)$

$P = a + b_1 + c + b_2$

1. $a =$ _____
$b =$ _____
$c =$ _____
$h =$ _____
$A =$ _____
$P =$ _____

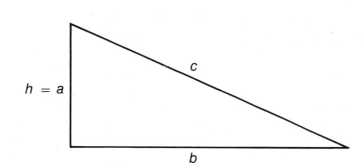

2. $a =$ _____
$b_1 =$ _____
$c =$ _____
$b_2 =$ _____
$h =$ _____
$A =$ _____
$P =$ _____

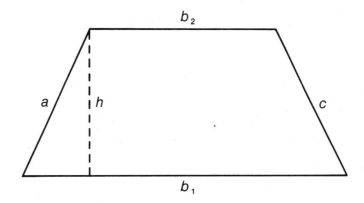

3. $a =$ _____
$b =$ _____
$h =$ _____
$A =$ _____
$P =$ _____

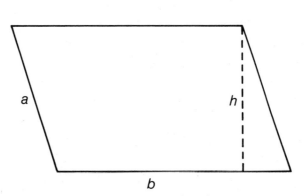

Triangles, parallelograms, and trapezoids

Measure the length of the sides and the altitude of each figure to the nearest millimeter. Find the area and perimeter of each. Be sure to write units in your answers.

Triangle

$A = \frac{1}{2} b \times h$

$P = a + b + c$

Parallelogram

$A = b \times h$

$P = 2a + 2b$

Trapezoid

$A = \frac{1}{2} h (b_1 + b_2)$

$P = a + b_1 + c + b_2$

1. $a =$ _____
$b =$ _____
$c =$ _____
$h =$ _____
$A =$ _____
$P =$ _____

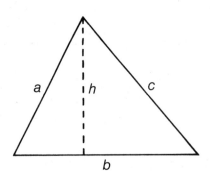

2. $a =$ _____
$b =$ _____
$h =$ _____
$A =$ _____
$P =$ _____

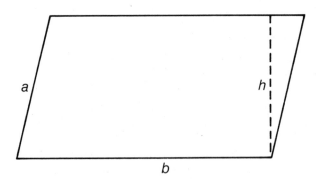

3. $a =$ _____
$b_1 =$ _____
$c =$ _____
$b_2 =$ _____
$h =$ _____
$A =$ _____
$P =$ _____

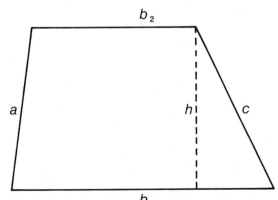

Quiz

Triangles, parallelograms, and trapezoids

Name _____

Date _____

Measure the length of the sides and the altitude of each figure to the nearest quarter-inch. Find the area and perimeter of each. Be sure to write units in your answers.

Triangle	Parallelogram	Trapezoid
$A = \frac{1}{2}b \times h$	$A = b \times h$	$A = \frac{1}{2}h(b_1 + b_2)$
$P = a + b + c$	$P = 2a + 2b$	$P = a + b_1 + c + b_2$

1. $a =$ _____

$b =$ _____

$h =$ _____

$A =$ _____

$P =$ _____

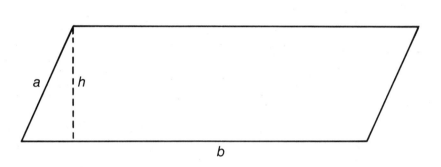

2. $a =$ _____

$b =$ _____

$c =$ _____

$h =$ _____

$A =$ _____

$P =$ _____

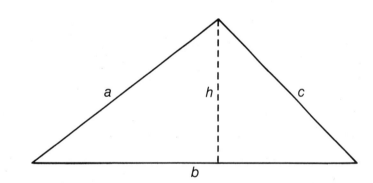

3. $a =$ _____

$b_1 =$ _____

$c =$ _____

$b_2 =$ _____

$h =$ _____

$A =$ _____

$P =$ _____

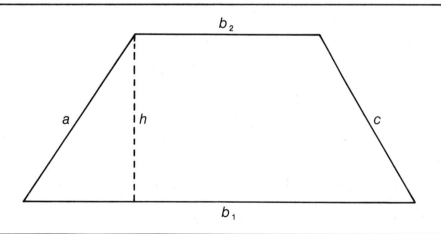

Quiz

Triangles, parallelograms, and trapezoids

Name _____

Date _____

Measure the length of the sides and the altitude of each figure to the nearest millimeter. Find the area and perimeter of each. Be sure to write units in your answers.

Triangle

$A = \frac{1}{2} b \times h$

$P = a + b + c$

Parallelogram

$A = b \times h$

$P = 2a + 2b$

Trapezoid

$A = \frac{1}{2} h (b_1 + b_2)$

$P = a + b_1 + c + b_2$

1. $a =$ _____
   $b =$ _____
   $c =$ _____
   $h =$ _____
   $A =$ _____
   $P =$ _____

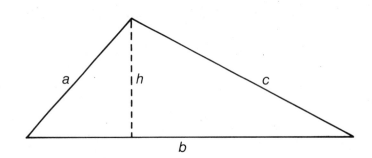

2. $a =$ _____
   $b =$ _____
   $h =$ _____
   $A =$ _____
   $P =$ _____

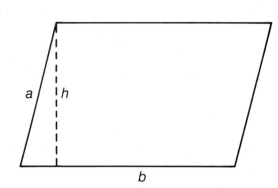

3. $a =$ _____
   $b_1 =$ _____
   $c =$ _____
   $b_2 =$ _____
   $h =$ _____
   $A =$ _____
   $P =$ _____

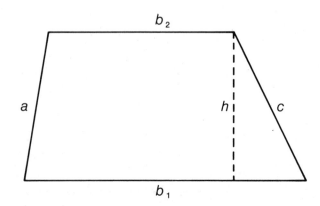

Quiz
Volume

Name _____

Date _____

Find each volume. Be sure to write units in your answers. Use 3.14 for π.

Cube	Rectangular Prism	Triangular Prism
$V = e^3$	$V = lwh$	$V = \frac{1}{2}abh$

Sphere	Cylinder	Cone
$V = \frac{4}{3}\pi r^3$	$V = \pi r^2 h$	$V = \frac{1}{3}\pi r^2 h$

1. Cube $e = 7$ in.	**2.** Rectangular Prism $l = 25$ ft $w = 17$ ft $h = 13$ ft	**3.** Triangular Prism $b = 13$ in. $a = 10$ in. $h = 5$ in.
4. Sphere $r = 45$ ft	**5.** Cylinder $r = 38$ in. $h = 13$ in.	**6.** Cone $r = 150$ in. $h = 85$ in.

Quiz
Volume

Name _____
Date _____

Find each volume. Be sure to write units in your answers. Use 3.14 for π.

Cube
$V = e^3$

Rectangular Prism
$V = lwh$

Triangular Prism
$V = \frac{1}{2}abh$

Sphere
$V = \frac{4}{3}\pi r^3$

Cylinder
$V = \pi r^2 h$

Cone
$V = \frac{1}{3}\pi r^2 h$

1. Cube $e = 13$ cm	2. Rectangular Prism $l = 17$ mm $w = 8$ mm $h = 6$ mm	3. Triangular Prism $b = 38$ cm $a = 12$ cm $h = 5$ cm
4. Sphere $r = 21$ m	5. Cylinder $r = 14$ cm $h = 12$ cm	6. Cone $r = 29$ mm $h = 12$ mm

Quiz
Volume

Name _____

Date _____

Find each volume. Be sure to write units in your answers. Use 3.14 for π.

Cube
$V = e^3$

Rectangular Prism
$V = lwh$

Triangular Prism
$V = \frac{1}{2}abh$

Sphere
$V = \frac{4}{3}\pi r^3$

Cylinder
$V = \pi r^2 h$

Cone
$V = \frac{1}{3}\pi r^2 h$

1. Cube $e = 11$ in.	**2.** Rectangular Prism $l = 16$ ft $w = 9$ ft $h = 3$ ft	**3.** Triangular Prism $b = 70$ in. $a = 25$ in. $h = 12$ in.
4. Sphere $r = 35$ in.	**5.** Cylinder $r = 42$ yd $h = 28$ yd	**6.** Cone $r = 49$ in. $h = 27$ in.

Quiz
Volume

Name _____

Date _____

Find each volume. Be sure to write units in your answers. Use 3.14 for π.

Cube	Rectangular Prism	Triangular Prism
$V = e^3$	$V = lwh$	$V = \frac{1}{2}abh$

Sphere	Cylinder	Cone
$V = \frac{4}{3}\pi r^3$	$V = \pi r^2 h$	$V = \frac{1}{3}\pi r^2 h$

1. Cube	2. Rectangular Prism	3. Triangular Prism
$e = 8$ mm	$l = 35$ cm $w = 22$ cm $h = 8$ cm	$b = 14$ m $a = 11$ m $h = 7$ m
4. Sphere	5. Cylinder	6. Cone
$r = 30$ cm	$r = 28$ cm $h = 9$ cm	$r = 16$ m $h = 15$ m

148

Name _____

Date _____

Find the radius, circumference, and area of each circle. Use 3.14 for π.

$r = \frac{1}{2}d$　　　　　　　$C = \pi d$　　　　　　　$A = \pi r^2$

1. $d = 50$ in.

$r =$ _____

$C =$ _____

$A =$ _____

2. $d = 38$ ft

$r =$ _____

$C =$ _____

$A =$ _____

3. $d = 4$ yd

$r =$ _____

$C =$ _____

$A =$ _____

4. $d = 30$ ft

$r =$ _____

$C =$ _____

$A =$ _____

5. $d = 15$ in.

$r =$ _____

$C =$ _____

$A =$ _____

Name _____

Date _____

Find the radius, circumference, and area of each circle. Use 3.14 for π.

$r = \frac{1}{2}d$ $\qquad\qquad\qquad$ $C = \pi d$ $\qquad\qquad\qquad$ $A = \pi r^2$

1. d = 34 mm

r = _____

C = _____

A = _____

2. d = 40 cm

r = _____

C = _____

A = _____

3. d = 20 dm

r = _____

C = _____

A = _____

4. d = 30 m

r = _____

C = _____

A = _____

5. d = 19 cm

r = _____

C = _____

A = _____

Name _____

Date _____

Find the radius, circumference, and area of each circle. Use 3.14 for π.

$r = \frac{1}{2}d$ $\qquad\qquad$ $C = \pi d$ $\qquad\qquad$ $A = \pi r^2$

1. $d = 50$ yd

$r =$ _____

$C =$ _____

$A =$ _____

2. $d = 32$ in.

$r =$ _____

$C =$ _____

$A =$ _____

3. $d = 18$ ft

$r =$ _____

$C =$ _____

$A =$ _____

4. $d = 52$ in.

$r =$ _____

$C =$ _____

$A =$ _____

5. $d = 45$ ft

$r =$ _____

$C =$ _____

$A =$ _____

Quiz

Circles

Name _____

Date _____

Find the radius, circumference, and area of each circle. Use 3.14 for π.

$r = \frac{1}{2}d$ $C = \pi d$ $A = \pi r^2$

---

1. $d = 5$ km

  $r =$ _____

  $C =$ _____

  $A =$ _____

---

2. $d = 60$ mm

  $r =$ _____

  $C =$ _____

  $A =$ _____

---

3. $d = 14$ dm

  $r =$ _____

  $C =$ _____

  $A =$ _____

---

4. $d = 76$ cm

  $r =$ _____

  $C =$ _____

  $A =$ _____

---

5. $d = 30$ m

  $r =$ _____

  $C =$ _____

  $A =$ _____

Quiz
Money

Name _____

Date _____

The purchase is to be taken out of $20. Determine the most efficient change.

1. Purchase: $9.72			2. Purchase: $16.81			3. Purchase: $12.57		
___ $10	___ 25¢		___ $10	___ 25¢		___ $10	___ 25¢	
___ $ 5	___ 10¢		___ $ 5	___ 10¢		___ $ 5	___ 10¢	
___ $ 1	___ 5¢		___ $ 1	___ 5¢		___ $ 1	___ 5¢	
___ 50¢	___ 1¢		___ 50¢	___ 1¢		___ 50¢	___ 1¢	

4. Purchase: $8.32			5. Purchase: $5.16			6. Purchase: $7.78		
___ $10	___ 25¢		___ $10	___ 25¢		___ $10	___ 25¢	
___ $ 5	___ 10¢		___ $ 5	___ 10¢		___ $ 5	___ 10¢	
___ $ 1	___ 5¢		___ $ 1	___ 5¢		___ $ 1	___ 5¢	
___ 50¢	___ 1¢		___ 50¢	___ 1¢		___ 50¢	___ 1¢	

Find the unit prices. Circle the best buy.

7. a. $1.43 for 13 oz	8. a. $ 29.25 for box of 25	9. a. $ 4.48 for 16 lb
b. $2.34 for 18 oz	b. $ 60.50 for box of 50	b. $11.25 for 45 lb
c. $3.36 for 32 oz	c. $118.00 for box of 100	c. $14.04 for 52 lb
10. a. $ 8.96 for 16 gal	11. a. $1.04 for 13 oz	12. a. $ 2.25 for 25 ft
b. $23.84 for 42 gal	b. $3.24 for 27 oz	b. $ 8.00 for 100 ft
c. $35.40 for 60 gal	c. $3.64 for 52 oz	c. $10.00 for 200 ft

153

Name _____

Date _____

The purchase is to be taken out of $20. Determine the most efficient change.

1. Purchase: $7.32	
_____ $10	_____ 25¢
_____ $ 5	_____ 10¢
_____ $ 1	_____ 5¢
_____ 50¢	_____ 1¢

2. Purchase: $15.57	
_____ $10	_____ 25¢
_____ $ 5	_____ 10¢
_____ $ 1	_____ 5¢
_____ 50¢	_____ 1¢

3. Purchase: $12.59	
_____ $10	_____ 25¢
_____ $ 5	_____ 10¢
_____ $ 1	_____ 5¢
_____ 50¢	_____ 1¢

4. Purchase: $3.68	
_____ $10	_____ 25¢
_____ $ 5	_____ 10¢
_____ $ 1	_____ 5¢
_____ 50¢	_____ 1¢

5. Purchase: $9.83	
_____ $10	_____ 25¢
_____ $ 5	_____ 10¢
_____ $ 1	_____ 5¢
_____ 50¢	_____ 1¢

6. Purchase: $7.97	
_____ $10	_____ 25¢
_____ $ 5	_____ 10¢
_____ $ 1	_____ 5¢
_____ 50¢	_____ 1¢

Find the unit prices. Circle the best buy.

7. a. $2.70 for 10 g	8. a. $ 3.75 for box of 25	9. a. $2.32 for 8 kg
b. $3.15 for 15 g	b. $ 6.00 for box of 50	b. $3.00 for 10 kg
c. $5.00 for 20 g	c. $10.00 for box of 100	c. $4.80 for 15 kg
10. a. $ 7.65 for 15 mL	11. a. $1.76 for 8 L	12. a. $ 4.50 for 50 m
b. $13.75 for 25 mL	b. $2.88 for 12 L	b. $ 6.00 for 75 m
c. $22.40 for 40 mL	c. $4.20 for 20 L	c. $10.00 for 100 m

Name _____

Date _____

The purchase is to be taken out of $20. Determine the most efficient change.

1. Purchase: $12.59	
_____ $10	_____ 25¢
_____ $ 5	_____ 10¢
_____ $ 1	_____ 5¢
_____ 50¢	_____ 1¢

2. Purchase: $7.83	
_____ $10	_____ 25¢
_____ $ 5	_____ 10¢
_____ $ 1	_____ 5¢
_____ 50¢	_____ 1¢

3. Purchase: $16.48	
_____ $10	_____ 25¢
_____ $ 5	_____ 10¢
_____ $ 1	_____ 5¢
_____ 50¢	_____ 1¢

4. Purchase: $4.07	
_____ $10	_____ 25¢
_____ $ 5	_____ 10¢
_____ $ 1	_____ 5¢
_____ 50¢	_____ 1¢

5. Purchase: $8.32	
_____ $10	_____ 25¢
_____ $ 5	_____ 10¢
_____ $ 1	_____ 5¢
_____ 50¢	_____ 1¢

6. Purchase: $14.81	
_____ $10	_____ 25¢
_____ $ 5	_____ 10¢
_____ $ 1	_____ 5¢
_____ 50¢	_____ 1¢

Find the unit prices. Circle the best buy.

7. a. $ 5.70 for 15 g b. $ 8.82 for 21 g c. $16.80 for 30 g	8. a. $3.00 for box of 100 b. $4.00 for box of 200 c. $7.50 for box of 500	9. a. $ 3.00 for 25 m b. $ 8.25 for 75 m c. $18.00 for 200 m
10. a. $ 6.30 for 18 mL b. $ 7.44 for 24 mL c. $12.48 for 48 mL	11. a. $2.30 for 125 kg b. $3.40 for 200 kg c. $8.00 for 200 kg	12. a. $ 2.25 for 15 m b. $ 5.10 for 30 m c. $11.04 for 48 m

155

Quiz
Money

Name _____

Date _____

The purchase is to be taken out of $20. Determine the most efficient change.

1. Purchase: $11.58		2. Purchase: $13.32		3. Purchase: $17.82	
_____ $10	_____ 25¢	_____ $10	_____ 25¢	_____ $10	_____ 25¢
_____ $ 5	_____ 10¢	_____ $ 5	_____ 10¢	_____ $ 5	_____ 10¢
_____ $ 1	_____ 5¢	_____ $ 1	_____ 5¢	_____ $ 1	_____ 5¢
_____ 50¢	_____ 1¢	_____ 50¢	_____ 1¢	_____ 50¢	_____ 1¢

4. Purchase: $9.28		5. Purchase: $7.85		6. Purchase: $9.61	
_____ $10	_____ 25¢	_____ $10	_____ 25¢	_____ $10	_____ 25¢
_____ $ 5	_____ 10¢	_____ $ 5	_____ 10¢	_____ $ 5	_____ 10¢
_____ $ 1	_____ 5¢	_____ $ 1	_____ 5¢	_____ $ 1	_____ 5¢
_____ 50¢	_____ 1¢	_____ 50¢	_____ 1¢	_____ 50¢	_____ 1¢

Find the unit prices. Circle the best buy.

7. a. $1.55 for 43	8. a. $4.14 for 23 oz	9. a. $ 4.55 for box of 35
b. $2.82 for 91	b. $7.92 for 36 oz	b. $12.60 for box of 90
c. $3.75 for 117	c. $9.88 for 52 oz	c. $15.40 for box of 140
10. a. $1.20 for 75 in.²	11. a. $0.77 for 35	12. a. $1.17 for 13 oz
b. $1.88 for 125 in.²	b. $1.08 for 60	b. $2.16 for 27 oz
c. $2.31 for 165 in.²	c. $2.10 for 100	c. $2.94 for 42 oz

Name _____

Date _____

Solve each problem.

---

1. A car dealer gave a $700 rebate on a $5800 car. To the nearest whole number, what percent rebate was this?

---

2. If the heart pumps 80 mL of blood each second, how many liters of blood does it pump each hour?

---

3. A cheetah, the fastest animal on earth, can run 70 miles per hour. How many feet per second is this?

---

4. The wheel of a bicycle has a 26-inch diameter. Each time the wheel turns a complete revolution, the bicycle moves a distance equal to the circumference of the wheel. How far has a rider traveled when the wheel has gone around 1000 times? (Use $\pi = 3.14$. Give the answer to the nearest foot.)

---

5. The population of Colorado was 3,407,209 one year. The state spent $7,598,076.07 on pollution control. What amount was spent per person?

---

6. At the sixty-eighth annual Millrose games, Francie Larrieu won the 1000-yard run with a time of 2 minutes 27 seconds. How fast did she run in miles per hour? (Give the answer to the nearest tenth.)

Name _____

Date _____

Solve each problem.

1. During his career as a football player, Don Meredith attempted 2308 passes and completed 1170. To the nearest whole percent, what percent of his passes were incomplete?

2. There were 510 points possible in a mathematics class for the semester. If Leigh had 90%, how many points had she missed during the semester?

3. Andreas worked 29 hours during the week at $4.57 per hour. Eighteen and one-half percent of his pay was withheld for social security, state disability insurance, and income tax. How much did he receive for his week's work?

4. Jolene's car gets 32 miles per gallon. She pays $1.56 per gallon for gasoline. How much did she spend for gasoline on a 2600 mile trip?

5. A vat in the shape of a cylinder has radius 5 feet and height 7 feet. It is to be filled with cleaning fluid. The cleaning fluid costs $26.75 per gallon. What will it cost to fill the tank? (1 ft³ = 7.48 gal. Use π = 3.14. Give the answer to the nearest dollar.)

6. Albert has 213 pine trees to be sprayed to control the pine beetle. Each gallon of spray costs $49.50 and mixes with water to make 40 gallons of spray. It takes $\frac{3}{4}$ gallons of spray for each tree. How much will it cost to spray all 213 trees? (Give the answer to the nearest dollar.)

Solve each problem.

---

1. Janice performed an experiment with her motorcycle at the local race track. In five tries it took 3.1 seconds, 3.0 seconds, 2.8 seconds, 3.6 seconds, and 2.9 seconds for her to accelerate to 20 miles per hour. What was the average time needed for the cycle to reach 20 miles per hour?

---

2. On a back packing trip, Carlos walked 16 kilometers per day for each of five days. He walked a total of 50 hours. What was his average rate of walking?

---

3. The outside walls of a rectangular-shaped warehouse are to be painted. The warehouse is 100 meters long, 90 meters wide, and 30 meters high and has no windows. One liter of paint covers 100 square meters. How many liters of paint will be needed?

---

4. Berta earned $700 on a $2500 investment over a two-year period. What rate of interest did she receive?

---

5. In one day of shopping Rick spent $29.75 on clothes, $16.50 in the supermarket and $14.00 at the bookstore. All these items were taxed at 6%. How much money did he have left out of $75.00?

---

6. A new car costs $8750, sales tax is $6\frac{1}{2}$% and the title and license together cost $173.50. What is the total cost of the car?

Name _____

Date _____

Solve each problem.

1. Barbara's grades on 10 tests were 83, 77, 96, 63, 89, 74, 80, 92, 67, and 81. What was the average of these grades?

2. Phil worked 40 hours at $8.75 an hour. He had deductions totaling $12.88. What was his net pay?

3. A coat bought on a 25% off sale cost $52.56. What was the original price of the coat?

4. A room measures 25 meters by 18 meters. It is to be covered with carpet priced at $12.50 a square meter. Find the cost of the carpet.

5. Trudy bought 5 items costing $6.95, $5.27, $12.52, $6.81, and $23.17, respectively. She paid 6% sales tax on these items. What was the total bill, including tax?

6. Bill drove his car 2100 kilometers and bought gasoline six times. The amounts of his gasoline purchases were $17.52, $21.43, $18.47, $19.62, $15.43, and $20.76. What was the average cost of his fuel per kilometer? (Give the answer to the nearest cent.)

Name _____

Date _____

Directions: Choose the most reasonable answer. Circle the letter of the answer.

1. Add. 509 37 628 4 <u>283</u>	A. 1431 B. 1441 C. 1461 D. None of these	
2. Find the sum of 695 and 8321.	A. 9016 B. 15,271 C. 8916 D. 8016	
3. Find the total. 1287 327 1483 6029 43 <u>7705</u>	A. 16,874 B. 16,854 C. 16,774 D. 15,874	
4. Add. 9011 7562 3881 <u>4625</u>	A. 25,089 B. 24,089 C. 25,079 D. None of these	
5. Subtract. 8057 <u>392</u>	A. 7665 B. 3421 C. 7645 D. 7765	
6. Subtract 3851 from 9836.	A. 5985 B. 6015 C. 6025 D. 6085	

Name _____

Date _____

Directions: Choose the most reasonable answer. Circle the letter of the answer.

7. 3068 − 447 = ?	A. 2521 B. 3421 C. 3521 D. 2621
8. Find the product of 67 and 53.	A. 3531 B. 3551 C. 3451 D. None of these
9. Multiply. 357 602	A. 22,134 B. 214,904 C. 216,114 D. 214,914
10. Multiply 608 by 275.	A. 167,180 B. 167,200 C. 18,700 D. 179,200
11. Divide. 53)2491	A. 407 B. 470 C. 47 D. None of these
12. Divide 15,035 by 5.	A. 307 B. 301 C. 3001 D. 3007
13. 13,626 ÷ 6 = ?	A. 2301 B. 2271 C. 11,271 D. 22,071
14. Add. $\frac{5}{12}$ $\frac{5}{8}$	A. $\frac{1}{2}$ B. $\frac{10}{20}$ C. $\frac{25}{48}$ D. $\frac{25}{24}$

Name _____

Date _____

Directions: Choose the most reasonable answer. Circle the letter of the answer.

---

15. Add $\frac{1}{4}$ and $\frac{5}{6}$.

A. $\frac{13}{12}$ B. $\frac{6}{10}$

C. $\frac{3}{5}$ D. $\frac{13}{14}$

---

16. Find the sum of $\frac{4}{5}$ and $\frac{7}{15}$.

A. $\frac{19}{15}$ B. $\frac{11}{20}$

C. $\frac{19}{30}$ D. None of these

---

17. Subtract $\frac{5}{8}$ from $\frac{7}{8}$.

A. $\frac{3}{2}$ B. $\frac{1}{4}$

C. $\frac{12}{8}$ D. $\frac{12}{16}$

---

18. Subtract $\frac{6}{7}$ from $\frac{11}{12}$.

A. $\frac{159}{84}$ B. $\frac{8}{42}$

C. $\frac{4}{21}$ D. $\frac{5}{84}$

---

19. $\frac{4}{5} \times \frac{20}{21} = ?$

A. $\frac{4}{7}$ B. $\frac{20}{21}$

C. $\frac{16}{21}$ D. $\frac{100}{105}$

---

20. Find the least common denominator for $\frac{7}{20}$ and $\frac{17}{24}$.

A. 80 B. 60

C. 120 D. 100

---

21. $\frac{5}{6} - \frac{3}{5} = ?$

A. $\frac{7}{30}$ B. $\frac{43}{30}$

C. $\frac{7}{60}$ D. $\frac{43}{60}$

---

22. $\frac{5}{12} \times \frac{10}{13} = ?$

A. $\frac{5}{26}$ B. $\frac{25}{78}$

C. $\frac{5}{13}$ D. None of these

Name _____

Date _____

Directions: Choose the most reasonable answer. Circle the letter of the answer.

---

23. $\frac{4}{9} \times \frac{15}{16} \times \frac{12}{25} = ?$

A. 5   B. $\frac{3}{5}$

C. $\frac{12}{15}$ D. $\frac{1}{5}$

---

24. Divide $\frac{8}{15}$ by 4.

A. $\frac{32}{15}$ B. $\frac{15}{32}$

C. $\frac{15}{2}$ D. $\frac{2}{15}$

---

25. $\frac{5}{6} \div \frac{7}{12} = ?$

A. $\frac{5}{14}$ B. $\frac{35}{72}$

C. $\frac{10}{7}$ D. None of these

---

26. $7 \div \frac{3}{7} = ?$

A. 3   B. $\frac{49}{3}$

C. $\frac{3}{49}$ D. $\frac{1}{3}$

---

27. Add. $12\frac{2}{7}$

$11\frac{3}{7}$
_____

A. $23\frac{5}{14}$ B. $23\frac{6}{49}$

C. $23\frac{5}{7}$ D. $23\frac{1}{7}$

---

28. Add $18\frac{1}{8}$ and $6\frac{3}{8}$.

A. $24\frac{1}{4}$ B. $24\frac{1}{2}$

C. $24\frac{1}{8}$ D. $24\frac{5}{8}$

---

29. Find the sum of $17\frac{1}{4}$ and $12\frac{1}{3}$.

A. $29\frac{2}{7}$ B. $29\frac{7}{12}$

C. 30   D. $29\frac{1}{12}$

---

30. Add. $8\frac{3}{5}$

$7\frac{2}{3}$
_____

A. $16\frac{1}{2}$ B. $15\frac{5}{8}$

C. $15\frac{2}{3}$ D. $16\frac{4}{15}$

Name _____

Date _____

Directions: Choose the most reasonable answer. Circle the letter of the answer.

31. Find the sum of $6\frac{5}{8}$ and $9\frac{7}{12}$.

    A. $15\frac{5}{24}$ B. $15\frac{12}{16}$

    C. $16\frac{5}{24}$ D. $15\frac{3}{4}$

32. Add. $12\frac{1}{6}$

             $7\frac{1}{12}$

    A. $20\frac{8}{18}$ B. $20\frac{1}{2}$

    C. $19\frac{2}{3}$ D. $19\frac{1}{4}$

33. Subtract. $16\frac{6}{7}$

               $4\frac{3}{7}$

    A. $11\frac{3}{7}$ B. $20\frac{2}{7}$

    C. $12\frac{3}{7}$ D. $21\frac{2}{7}$

34. Subtract $13\frac{7}{15}$ from $22\frac{5}{12}$.

    A. $9\frac{37}{60}$ B. $1\frac{19}{20}$

    C. $8\frac{37}{60}$ D. $8\frac{19}{20}$

35. Find the difference between $36\frac{4}{5}$ and $8\frac{1}{5}$.

    A. $27\frac{3}{4}$ B. $27\frac{3}{5}$

    C. $28\frac{3}{5}$ D. $28\frac{3}{20}$

36. Subtract. $23\frac{1}{6}$

               $7\frac{3}{4}$

    A. $15\frac{1}{2}$ B. $16\frac{7}{12}$

    C. $16\frac{5}{12}$ D. $15\frac{5}{12}$

37. Subtract 8 from $35\frac{5}{7}$.

    A. $27\frac{5}{7}$ B. $26\frac{2}{7}$

    C. 27   D. None of these

38. Find the difference between 42 and $8\frac{9}{10}$.

    A. $34\frac{9}{10}$ B. $34\frac{1}{10}$

    C. $33\frac{9}{10}$ D. $33\frac{1}{10}$

Name _____

Date _____

Directions: Choose the most reasonable answer. Circle the letter of the answer.

39. $13\frac{3}{5} \times 6\frac{1}{4} = ?$	A. 85 B. 80 C. 78 D. $\frac{17}{5}$
40. $2\frac{5}{14} \times 9\frac{1}{3} = ?$	A. $\frac{11}{2}$ B. 22 C. $\frac{44}{6}$ D. $\frac{2}{11}$
41. $8\frac{1}{6} \times 2\frac{1}{7} = ?$	A. $\frac{35}{2}$ B. 14 C. 16 D. None of these
42. $4\frac{3}{8} \times 4\frac{2}{7} = ?$	A. $\frac{120}{7}$ B. 5 C. 15 D. $\frac{75}{4}$
43. $10\frac{3}{5} \times 1\frac{5}{7} = ?$	A. $\frac{96}{5}$ B. $\frac{636}{35}$ C. $\frac{120}{7}$ D. $\frac{53}{7}$
44. $4\frac{4}{5} \times 5\frac{2}{3} \times 4\frac{3}{8} = ?$	A. 119 B. $\frac{7}{17}$ C. 109 D. $\frac{8}{17}$
45. $4\frac{1}{2} \div 4\frac{1}{2} = ?$	A. 0 B. $\frac{81}{4}$ C. 11 D. 1
46. $3\frac{3}{16} \div 4\frac{1}{4} = ?$	A. $\frac{3}{16}$ B. $\frac{3}{17}$ C. $\frac{4}{17}$ D. $\frac{3}{4}$

Name _____

Date _____

Directions: Choose the most reasonable answer. Circle the letter of the answer.

---

47. $8\frac{1}{10} \div 7\frac{1}{5} = ?$

    A. $\frac{4}{5}$ B. $\frac{8}{9}$

    C. $\frac{5}{4}$ D. $\frac{9}{8}$

---

48. $14\frac{2}{7} \div 3\frac{3}{14} = ?$

    A. $\frac{40}{9}$ B. $\frac{2}{9}$

    C. $\frac{20}{9}$ D. $\frac{10}{9}$

---

49. $5\frac{10}{13} \div 1\frac{7}{26} = ?$

    A. $\frac{25}{11}$ B. $\frac{50}{11}$

    C. $\frac{22}{25}$ D. $\frac{150}{429}$

---

50. $9\frac{3}{5} \div 3\frac{6}{25} = ?$

    A. $\frac{5}{27}$ B. $\frac{16}{27}$

    C. $\frac{80}{27}$ D. $\frac{242}{81}$

---

51. Write $\frac{5}{8}$ as a decimal.

    A. $1.\overline{6}$ B. 0.625

    C. 62.5 D. $0.\overline{16}$

---

52. Write $\frac{3}{7}$ as a decimal.

    A. 0.12574 B. 0.428571

    C. $0.\overline{12574}$ D. $0.\overline{428571}$

---

53. Write 0.84 as a reduced fraction.

    A. $\frac{84}{100}$ B. $\frac{21}{25}$

    C. $\frac{3}{5}$ D. $\frac{12}{30}$

---

54. Write 1.825 as a reduced fraction.

    A. $\frac{1825}{1000}$ B. $\frac{365}{200}$

    C. $\frac{73}{40}$ D. None of these

Name _____

Date _____

Directions: Choose the most reasonable answer. Circle the letter of the answer.

---

55. Solve for x.　　　　$\frac{5}{9} = \frac{x}{36}$

　　A. $x = 20$　　B. $x = 10$

　　C. $x = 40$　　D. None of these

---

56. Solve for x.　　　　$\frac{25}{x} = \frac{5}{13}$

　　A. $x = 58$　　　B. $x = 10$

　　C. $x = 130$　　D. $x = 65$

---

57. $7.635 + 0.67 + 8 + 2.4 = ?$

　　A. 18.605　　B. 11.505

　　C. 18.705　　D. 11.405

---

58. Find the sum of 4.37, 6.2, 36.751, and 500.4.

　　A. 547.621　　B. 547.721

　　C. 546.721　　D. 647.721

---

59. Add.　　　　5.92
　　　　　　　　　7.3
　　　　　　　　　0.601
　　　　　　　　　0.0047

　　A. 13.8267　　B. 13.8257

　　C. 12.8257　　D. 13.8267

---

60. Subtract 6.098 from 8.2036.

　　A. 2.2056　　B. 2.8956

　　C. 1.8956　　D. 2.1056

---

61. Subtract.　　　　12.7
　　　　　　　　　　　8.391

　　A. 4.409　　B. 4.491

　　C. 4.309　　D. 5.491

---

62. Subtract 3 from 16.87.

　　A. 16.84　　B. 16.57

　　C. 13.87　　D. None of these

Name _____

Date _____

Directions: Choose the most reasonable answer. Circle the letter of the answer.

63. Multiply.	$\begin{array}{r} 0.86 \\ \underline{0.47} \end{array}$	A. 0.004042	B. 40.42
		C. 4042	D. 0.4042

64. Multiply 16.72 by 7.6.
    A. 127.072   B. 1270.72
    C. 127.062   D. 1270.62

65. Multiply 0.056 by 0.4.
    A. 0.0224   B. 0.224
    C. 22.4   D. 0.0204

66. Divide.

$0.67\overline{)542.164}$

    A. 809.2   B. 89.2
    C. 8.92   D. 80.92

67. Round 821.649 to the nearest tenth.
    A. 821.7   B. 821.6
    C. 821.600   D. 821.65

68. $877.39 \div 100 = ?$
    A. 87.739   B. 87,739
    C. 8.7739   D. 8773.9

69. Divide 7.5808 by 0.92.
    A. 8.24   B. 0.824
    C. 82.4   D. 0.0824

70. Divide.

$3.6\overline{)2898}$

    A. 85   B. 805
    C. 8.5   D. 80.5

Name _____

Date _____

Directions: Choose the most reasonable answer. Circle the letter of the answer.

71. Reduce $\frac{14}{105}$ to lowest terms.	A. $\frac{14}{105}$ B. $\frac{2}{15}$ C. $\frac{2}{17}$ D. $\frac{1}{7}$
72. Multiply 36.952 by 100.	A. 3.6952 B. 0.36952 C. 369.52 D. 3695.2
73. List all the divisors of 36.	A. 1, 2, 3, 6, 9, 12, 18, 36 B. 2, 3, 4, 6, 9, 12, 18 C. 1, 2, 3, 4, 6, 9, 12, 18, 36 D. 1, 2, 3, 4, 6, 8, 9, 12, 18, 36
74. Write 24 as the product of prime numbers.	A. $2 \times 2 \times 6$ B. 2×12 C. $2 \times 2 \times 2 \times 3$ D. None of these
75. Write in order from smallest to largest: $\frac{1}{2}, \frac{1}{3}, \frac{3}{4}$	A. $\frac{3}{4}, \frac{1}{3}, \frac{1}{2}$ B. $\frac{1}{2}, \frac{1}{3}, \frac{3}{4}$ C. $\frac{3}{4}, \frac{1}{2}, \frac{1}{3}$ D. $\frac{1}{3}, \frac{1}{2}, \frac{3}{4}$
76. Find the gross pay for 37 hours at $3.57 per hour.	A. $121.09 B. $131.09 C. $132.09 D. $129.69
77. Find the net pay if the gross pay is $157.23 and deductions are $12.51.	A. $144.72 B. $169.74 C. $145.32 D. $145.72
78. Write 17% as a decimal.	A. 0.17% B. 0.17 C. 1.7 D. 1.7%

Directions: Choose the most reasonable answer. Circle the letter of the answer.

---

79. Write 42.3% as a decimal.

A. 0.423   B. 0.423%

C. 4.23   D. 4.23%

---

80. Write 1.67% as a decimal.

A. 0.0167   B. 0.0167%

C. 16.7   D. 16.7%

---

81. Write 0.07 as a percent.

A. 70%   B. 0.007%

C. 7%   D. 700%

---

82. Write 2.5 as a percent.

A. 0.25%   B. 25%

C. 250%   D. 2.5%

---

83. Write 0.16 as a percent.

A. 1.6%   B. 16%

C. 160%   D. 0.016%

---

84. Write $\frac{1}{8}$ as a percent.

A. 125%   B. 12.5%

C. 8%   D. 80%

---

85. Write $\frac{2}{3}$ as a percent.

A. $66\frac{2}{3}$%   B. $33\frac{1}{3}$%

C. 23%   D. 67%

---

86. Write $\frac{3}{5}$ as a percent.

A. 40%   B. 60%

C. 35%   D. 350%

Name _____

Date _____

Directions: Choose the most reasonable answer. Circle the letter of the answer.

87. 15 is what percent of 30?	A. 50% B. $\frac{1}{2}$% C. 5% D. 200%
88. 4 is what percent of 16?	A. 4% B. $\frac{1}{4}$% C. 25% D. 400%
89. 8 is what percent of 12?	A. 23% B. 150% C. $33\frac{1}{3}$% D. $66\frac{2}{3}$%
90. 7 is what percent of 21?	A. $\frac{1}{3}$% B. $33\frac{1}{3}$% C. 33% D. 3%
91. Find 16% of 12.	A. 1.92 B. 192 C. 19.2 D. 0.192
92. What number is 18% of 63?	A. 11.34 B. 1.134 C. 113.4 D. None of these
93. 62% of 47 = ?	A. 29.14 B. 2.914 C. 291.4 D. 2914
94. Find $33\frac{1}{3}$% of 33.	A. $1\frac{1}{3}$ B. 11 C. 3 D. 99

Directions: Choose the most reasonable answer. Circle the letter of the answer.

95. 30 is 12% of what number?

A. $2\frac{1}{2}$ B. 3.5

C. 250   D. $\frac{2}{5}$

96. 45 is 90% of what number?

A. $\frac{1}{2}$ B. 40.5

C. 2   D. 50

97. 8.71 is 13% of what number?

A. 670   B. 1.1323

C. 67   D. 11.323

98. Find the interest on $5000 at 8% for one year.

A. $40,000   B. $400

C. $40   D. $4000

99. A refrigerator priced at $396 is marked at $132 off the regular price. What is the rate of discount?

A. 33%   B. $66\frac{2}{3}$%

C. 50%   D. $33\frac{1}{3}$%

100. The profit on furniture at the Accent Furniture Store is 25% of the cost to the store. The profit on a dresser is $75. What did the dresser cost the store?

A. $3000   B. $18.75

C. $300   D. $187.50

Name _____

Date _____

Directions: Choose the most reasonable answer. Circle the letter of the answer.

1. Add.   726
          92
      568
        9
     243
	A. 1538 B. 1628
	C. 1638 D. 1528	

2. Find the sum of 742 and 9654.

A. 10,396   B. 10,406
C. 9396   D. 10,496

3. Find the total.   3822
                  416
               5376
               8026
                  47
               7615

A. 24,302   B. 25,282
C. 25,302   D. 24,282

4. Add.   6966
          4321
         8207
         6935

A. 26,429   B. 25,429
C. 26,419   D. 25,419

5. Subtract.   7652
            487

A. 7165   B. 7175
C. 7164   D. 6165

6. Subtract 2557 from 7352.

A. 4805   B. 4795
C. 4894   D. 4794

Name _____

Date _____

Directions: Choose the most reasonable answer. Circle the letter of the answer.

7. 8307 − 695 = ?	A. 8702 B. 7702 C. 7612 D. 7712
8. Find the product of 32 and 79.	A. 2528 B. 111 C. 47 D. None of these
9. Multiply. 381 905	A. 333,805 B. 38,195 C. 343,805 D. 344,805
10. Multiply 509 by 324.	A. 19,216 B. 19,116 C. 165,916 D. 164,916
11. Divide. $42\overline{)2730}$	A. 605 B. 65 C. 650 D. 6050
12. Divide 36,072 by 9.	A. 480 B. 408 C. 48 D. 4008
13. 32,877 ÷ 9 = ?	A. 36,503 B. 36,053 C. 3653 D. 36,530
14. Add. $\frac{2}{9}$ $\frac{4}{9}$	A. $\frac{2}{3}$ B. $\frac{1}{3}$ C. $\frac{11}{13}$ D. $\frac{8}{9}$

Name _____

Date _____

Directions: Choose the most reasonable answer. Circle the letter of the answer.

---

15. Add $\frac{7}{10}$ and $\frac{7}{15}$.

   A. $\frac{7}{30}$ B. $\frac{7}{6}$

   C. $\frac{7}{12}$ D. $\frac{7}{60}$

---

16. Find the sum of $\frac{5}{8}$ and $\frac{7}{24}$.

   A. $\frac{1}{3}$ B. $\frac{3}{8}$

   C. $\frac{11}{12}$ D. $\frac{1}{6}$

---

17. Subtract $\frac{8}{21}$ from $\frac{6}{7}$.

   A. $\frac{1}{2}$ B. $\frac{26}{21}$

   C. $\frac{10}{21}$ D. $\frac{2}{5}$

---

18. Subtract $\frac{5}{12}$ from $\frac{4}{5}$.

   A. $\frac{73}{60}$ B. $\frac{23}{60}$

   C. $\frac{27}{60}$ D. $\frac{9}{20}$

---

19. $\frac{5}{6} \times \frac{18}{35} = ?$

   A. $\frac{3}{7}$ B. $\frac{1}{21}$

   C. $\frac{90}{210}$ D. None of these

---

20. Find the least common denominator for $\frac{9}{35}$ and $\frac{7}{30}$.

   A. 120   B. 65

   C. 5   D. 210

---

21. $\frac{3}{4} - \frac{2}{3} = ?$

   A. $\frac{1}{12}$ B. $\frac{5}{12}$

   C. $\frac{1}{4}$ D. $\frac{1}{3}$

---

22. $\frac{2}{9} \times \frac{6}{7} = ?$

   A. $\frac{1}{2}$ B. $\frac{6}{21}$

   C. $\frac{3}{7}$ D. $\frac{4}{21}$

Semester Test 1, Form B   Name _____
                              Date _____

Directions: Choose the most reasonable answer. Circle the letter of the answer.

23. $\frac{8}{21} \times \frac{14}{17} \times \frac{13}{20} = ?$

    A. $\frac{13}{85}$ B. $\frac{13}{255}$

    C. $\frac{52}{51}$ D. $\frac{52}{255}$

24. Divide $\frac{12}{17}$ by 6.

    A. $\frac{72}{17}$ B. $\frac{2}{17}$

    C. $\frac{3}{17}$ D. $\frac{84}{17}$

25. $\frac{2}{5} \div \frac{7}{10} = ?$

    A. $\frac{7}{25}$ B. $\frac{4}{7}$

    C. $\frac{7}{5}$ D. $\frac{7}{4}$

26. $9 \div \frac{5}{9} = ?$

    A. $\frac{1}{5}$ B. 5

    C. $\frac{81}{5}$ D. $\frac{5}{81}$

27. Add. $19\frac{2}{15}$ $8\frac{7}{15}$

    A. $28\frac{9}{30}$ B. $28\frac{3}{5}$

    C. $27\frac{9}{30}$ D. $27\frac{3}{5}$

28. Add $14\frac{7}{10}$ and $13\frac{9}{10}$.

    A. $28\frac{3}{5}$ B. $27\frac{3}{5}$

    C. $27\frac{16}{20}$ D. $27\frac{4}{5}$

29. Find the sum of $12\frac{5}{8}$ and $4\frac{3}{7}$.

    A. $16\frac{15}{36}$ B. $16\frac{8}{15}$

    C. $17\frac{3}{56}$ D. None of these

30. Add. $31\frac{3}{4}$ $9\frac{3}{5}$

    A. $40\frac{9}{20}$ B. $40\frac{6}{9}$

    C. $40\frac{2}{3}$ D. $41\frac{7}{20}$

Name _____

Date _____

Directions: Choose the most reasonable answer. Circle the letter of the answer.

---

31. Find the sum of $18\frac{7}{10}$ and $8\frac{7}{12}$.

    A. $26\frac{49}{120}$ B. $26\frac{14}{22}$

    C. $26\frac{7}{11}$ D. $27\frac{17}{60}$

---

32. Add.

    $24\frac{9}{16}$

    $14\frac{7}{12}$

    A. $38\frac{63}{192}$ B. $38\frac{16}{28}$

    C. $38\frac{4}{7}$ D. $39\frac{7}{48}$

---

33. Subtract.

    $12\frac{7}{8}$

    $7\frac{5}{8}$

    A. $5\frac{1}{8}$ B. $5\frac{2}{16}$

    C. $5\frac{1}{4}$ D. $4\frac{1}{8}$

---

34. Subtract 14 from $29\frac{3}{5}$.

    A. $14\frac{2}{5}$ B. $15\frac{3}{5}$

    C. $15\frac{2}{4}$ D. None of these

---

35. Find the difference between $34\frac{2}{3}$ and $7\frac{3}{4}$.

    A. $27\frac{5}{12}$ B. $27\frac{11}{12}$

    C. $26\frac{1}{12}$ D. $26\frac{11}{12}$

---

36. Subtract.

    $86\frac{5}{7}$

    $53\frac{5}{6}$

    A. $32\frac{37}{42}$ B. $32\frac{5}{42}$

    C. $33\frac{5}{42}$ D. $33\frac{37}{42}$

---

37. Subtract $11\frac{5}{8}$ from 19.

    A. $8\frac{3}{8}$ B. $8\frac{5}{8}$

    C. $7\frac{3}{8}$ D. $7\frac{5}{8}$

---

38. Find the difference between $27\frac{3}{10}$ and $12\frac{7}{15}$.

    A. $14\frac{5}{6}$ B. $15\frac{1}{6}$

    C. $15\frac{5}{30}$ D. $15\frac{5}{6}$

Directions: Choose the most reasonable answer. Circle the letter of the answer.

---

39. $5\frac{11}{14} \times 3\frac{8}{9} = ?$

    A. $22\frac{1}{2}$ B. $15\frac{44}{63}$

    C. 22 D. $8\frac{17}{23}$

---

40. $3\frac{15}{16} \times 5\frac{1}{7} = ?$

    A. $8\frac{16}{23}$ B. $15\frac{15}{112}$

    C. $20\frac{1}{4}$ D. None of these

---

41. $3\frac{3}{17} \times 7\frac{1}{12} = ?$

    A. 27 B. $21\frac{1}{68}$

    C. $10\frac{4}{29}$ D. $22\frac{1}{2}$

---

42. $4\frac{8}{15} \times 2\frac{5}{8} = ?$

    A. $8\frac{1}{3}$ B. $11\frac{9}{10}$

    C. $6\frac{13}{23}$ D. 12

---

43. $3\frac{15}{26} \times 7\frac{2}{9} = ?$

    A. $21\frac{5}{39}$ B. $25\frac{5}{6}$

    C. 31 D. $10\frac{17}{35}$

---

44. $2\frac{6}{7} \times 2\frac{2}{15} \times 3\frac{1}{16} = ?$

    A. $18\frac{2}{3}$ B. $12\frac{1}{140}$

    C. $7\frac{9}{38}$ D. None of these

---

45. $4\frac{8}{15} \div 6\frac{4}{5} = ?$

    A. $\frac{9}{4}$ B. $\frac{3}{2}$

    C. $\frac{4}{9}$ D. $\frac{2}{3}$

---

46. $2\frac{1}{10} \div 1\frac{24}{25} = ?$

    A. $\frac{14}{15}$ B. $\frac{15}{14}$

    C. $\frac{10}{161}$ D. $\frac{161}{10}$

Name _____

Date _____

Directions: Choose the most reasonable answer. Circle the letter of the answer.

---

47. $8\frac{1}{10} \div 1\frac{7}{20} = ?$

    A. $8\frac{2}{7}$ B. $\frac{1}{6}$

    C. 6   D. $\frac{82}{7}$

---

48. $6\frac{7}{9} \div 6\frac{7}{9} = ?$

    A. 10   B. $\frac{61}{81}$

    C. $1\frac{21}{60}$ D. 1

---

49. $2\frac{20}{21} \div 4\frac{3}{7} = ?$

    A. $\frac{3}{2}$ B. $\frac{2}{3}$

    C. $\frac{20}{49}$ D. $\frac{10}{49}$

---

50. $6\frac{4}{9} \div 9\frac{2}{3} = ?$

    A. $\frac{2}{3}$ B. $\frac{3}{2}$

    C. $15\frac{8}{27}$ D. $54\frac{8}{27}$

---

51. Write $\frac{7}{12}$ as a decimal.

    A. 0.583 B. $0.58\overline{3}$

    C. $0.\overline{583}$ D. $0.5\overline{83}$

---

52. Write $\frac{7}{16}$ as a decimal.

    A. $0.437\overline{5}$ B. 0.4375

    C. 0.4 D. $2.\overline{285714}$

---

53. Write 3.64 as a reduced fraction.

    A. $\frac{18}{5}$ B. $\frac{364}{100}$

    C. $\frac{91}{25}$ D. None of these

---

54. Write 0.128 as a reduced fraction.

    A. $\frac{4}{17}$ B. $\frac{128}{1000}$

    C. $\frac{8}{75}$ D. $\frac{16}{125}$

Name _____

Date _____

Directions: Choose the most reasonable answer. Circle the letter of the answer.

55. Solve for x. $\quad\frac{3}{17} = \frac{39}{x}$	A. $x = 42$ B. $x = 20$ C. $x = 221$ D. $x = 56$
56. Solve for x. $\quad\frac{x}{92} = \frac{11}{4}$	A. $x = 103$ B. $x = 253$ C. $x = 28$ D. $x = 96$
57. $23.4 + 0.45 + 12 + 6.3 = ?$	A. 27.984 B. 42.15 C. 10.434 D. 22.314
58. Find the sum of 9.2, 6.75, 400.9 and 63.475.	A. 417.38475 B. 83.433 C. 480.325 D. None of these

59. Add.   5.96
              8.3
            0.707
          0.0067
	A. 14.9737 B. 14.9637
	 C. 13.9737 D. 13.9637

60. Subtract 4.709 from 7.0042.	A. 3.7052 B. 2.2952 C. 2.3052 D. 3.3052
61. Subtract. 14.2 7.876	A. 7.476 B. 6.476 C. 6.324 D. 7.324
62. Subtract 6 from 19.21.	A. 18.41 B. 18.61 C. 19.61 D. 13.21

Name _____

Date _____

Directions: Choose the most reasonable answer. Circle the letter of the answer.

63. Multiply. $\quad$ 0.92 $\quad$ $\underline{0.37}$	A. 0.3594 $\quad$ B. 0.3394	C. 0.3504 $\quad$ D. 0.3404

64. Multiply 18.34 by 8.4.

A. 144.056 $\quad$ B. 154.046

C. 154.056 $\quad$ D. 144.046

65. Multiply 0.032 by 0.8.

A. 2.56 $\quad$ B. 0.256

C. 0.00256 $\quad$ D. 0.0256

66. Divide.

$$0.82\overline{)579.494}$$

A. 76.7 $\quad$ B. 706.7

C. 7067 $\quad$ D. 70.67

67. $3825.6 \div 100 = ?$

A. 38,256 $\quad$ B. 3,825,600

C. 382.52 $\quad$ D. 38.256

68. Divide 5.7685 by 0.83.

A. 6.95 $\quad$ B. 0.695

C. 69.5 $\quad$ D. 695

69. Divide 1666 by 2.8.

A. 595 $\quad$ B. 59.5

C. 5.95 $\quad$ D. 59.05

70. Reduce $\frac{20}{120}$ to lowest terms.

A. $\frac{1}{5}$ $\quad$ B. $\frac{1}{6}$

C. $\frac{2}{12}$ $\quad$ D. $\frac{4}{24}$

Name _____

Date _____

Directions: Choose the most reasonable answer. Circle the letter of the answer.

71. Multiply 8.321 by 1000.	A. 83.21 B. 832.1 C. 8321 D. 8.321
72. List all the divisors of 40.	A. 2, 4, 5, 8, 10, 20 B. 1, 2, 4, 5, 8, 10, 20, 40 C. 1, 2, 4, 10, 20, 40 D. 2, 4, 10, 20
73. Write 72 as the product of prime numbers.	A. $2 \times 2 \times 2 \times 3 \times 3$ B. $2 \times 2 \times 3 \times 3$ C. $2 \times 2 \times 2 \times 3$ D. 8×9
74. Round 467.537 to the nearest hundredth.	A. 467.54 B. 467.5 C. 467.540 D. 467.53
75. Write in order from smallest to largest: $\frac{3}{5}, \frac{5}{8}, \frac{6}{7}$	A. $\frac{6}{7}, \frac{5}{8}, \frac{3}{5}$ B. $\frac{5}{8}, \frac{3}{5}, \frac{6}{7}$ C. $\frac{3}{5}, \frac{5}{8}, \frac{6}{7}$ D. $\frac{6}{7}, \frac{3}{5}, \frac{5}{8}$
76. Find the gross pay for 35 hours at $4.25 per hour.	A. $148.75 B. $138.75 C. $158.75 D. None of these
77. Find the net pay if the gross pay is $139.62 and deductions are $14.27.	A. $153.89 B. $125.35 C. $115.35 D. $143.89
78. Write 3.5% as a decimal.	A. 0.35 B. 3.5 C. 350 D. 0.035

Directions: Choose the most reasonable answer. Circle the letter of the answer.

79. Write 53.4% as a decimal.	A. 53.4 B. 0.534 C. 0.0534 D. 5340
80. Write 1.82% as a decimal.	A. 0.182 B. 18.2 C. 1820 D. 0.0182
81. Write 0.08 as a percent.	A. 8% B. 80% C. 0.08% D. 0.8%
82. Write 7.2 as a percent.	A. 0.072% B. 720% C. 72% D. 0.72%
83. Write 0.43 as a percent.	A. 43% B. 0.43% C. 4.3% D. 430%
84. Write $\frac{3}{4}$ as a percent.	A. 125% B. 0.75% C. 75% D. 1.25%
85. Write $\frac{2}{9}$ as a percent.	A. 0.45% B. 22% C. $22\frac{2}{9}$% D. 4.5%
86. Write $\frac{5}{8}$ as a percent.	A. 160% B. 0.625% C. 16% D. $62\frac{1}{2}$%

Directions: Choose the most reasonable answer. Circle the letter of the answer.

87. 16 is what percent of 40?	A. $\frac{2}{5}$% B. 16% C. 40% D. 250%
88. 20 is what percent of 60?	A. 20% B. $33\frac{1}{3}$% C. $\frac{1}{3}$% D. 300%
89. 15 is what percent of 9?	A. $66\frac{2}{3}$% B. 60% C. 15% D. $166\frac{2}{3}$%
90. 32 is what percent of 96?	A. 300% B. $\frac{1}{3}$% C. $33\frac{1}{3}$% D. 32%
91. Find 12% of 63.	A. 7.56 B. 75.6 C. 5.25 D. 52.5
92. Find 126% of 45.	A. 2.8 B. 5670 C. 0.567 D. 56.7
93. Find 6.7% of 43.	A. 2.881 B. 28.81 C. 0.02881 D. 288.1
94. Find 80% of 75.	A. 0.6 B. 60 C. 25 D. 93.75

Name _____

Date _____

Directions: Choose the most reasonable answer. Circle the letter of the answer.

95. 162 is 45% of what number?	A. 7290 B. 72.9 C. 3.6 D. 360
96. 75 is 150% of what number?	A. 50 B. 112.5 C. 11,250 D. 500
97. 11.52 is 72% of what number?	A. 16 B. 8.2944 C. 0.16 D. 829.44
98. Find the interest on $4850 at 9% for one year.	A. $538.88 B. $436.50 C. $4365.00 D. $53.88
99. The regular price of a pair of shoes is $45. From this price $9 is marked off. What is the rate of discount?	A. 40.5% B. 405% C. 20% D. 54%
100. An automobile is sale priced at $4320. This is 90% of the original price. What was the original price?	A. $43,200 B. $3888 C. $4800 D. $5000

Name _____

Date _____

Directions: Choose the most reasonable answer. Circle the letter of the answer.

1. Measure to the nearest millimeter. _____	A. 2.7 mm B. 4.3 mm C. 27 mm D. 43 mm
2. Measure to the nearest tenth-centimeter. _____	A. 5.4 cm B. 54 cm C. 0.54 cm D. 540 cm
3. 280 m = ? km	A. 2800 B. 0.280 C. 2.8 D. 28
4. 47 cm = ? m	A. 4.7 B. 4700 C. 0.47 D. 0.0047
5. 147 mm = ? cm	A. 1.47 B. 0.147 C. 14.7 D. 1470
6. 3.83 m = ? mm	A. 0.383 B. 3830 C. 38.3 D. 383
7. $4\frac{1}{2}$ hours = ? minutes	A. 270 B. 450 C. $\frac{3}{40}$ D. $\frac{5}{6}$
8. 301 days = ? weeks	A. $75\frac{1}{4}$ B. 217 C. 43 D. $12\frac{13}{24}$

Directions: Choose the most reasonable answer. Circle the letter of the answer.

9. Add. 3 hr 50 min 5 hr 55 min	A. 9 hr 15 min B. 8 hr 15 min C. 8 hr 45 min D. 9 hr 45 min
10. Add. 6 mo 3 wk 15 days 3 mo 3 wk 6 days	A. 9 mo 1 wk B. 11 mo 1 wk C. 10 mo 1 wk D. 12 mo 1 wk 3 days
11. Subtract. 17 hr 32 min 12 hr 48 min	A. 4 hr 12 min B. 5 hr 12 min C. 5 hr 44 min D. 4 hr 44 min
12. Subtract. 12 yr 3 mo 2 wk 8 yr 11 mo 5 wk	A. 4 yr 8 mo 3 wk B. 3 yr 2 mo 7 wk C. 4 yr 3 mo 1 wk D. 3 yr 3 mo 1 wk
13. 60°C = ? °F	A. 140 B. $15\frac{5}{9}$ C. 92 D. $51\frac{1}{9}$
14. 59°F = ? °C	A. $50\frac{5}{9}$ B. 132.2 C. 15 D. 163.8
15. Find the measure of ∠A. 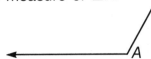	A. 60° B. 120° C. 95° D. 165°
16. Find the measure of ∠B. 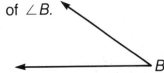	A. 35° B. 145° C. 90° D. 175°

Semester Test 2, Form A   Name _____

Date _____

Directions: Choose the most reasonable answer. Circle the letter of the answer.

17. ∠C and ∠D are complementary angles.
∠C measures 47°. Find the measure of ∠D.

A. 43°   B. 133°
C. 137°   D. 94°

18. ∠E and ∠F are complementary angles.
∠E measures 18°. Find the measure of ∠F.

A. 108°   B. 162°
C. 72°   D. 136°

19. ∠G and ∠H are supplementary angles.
∠G measures 25°. Find the measure of ∠H.

A. 155°   B. 65°
C. 115°   D. 50°

20. ∠J and ∠K are supplementary angles.
∠J measures 76°. Find the measure of ∠K.

A. 166°   B. 14°
C. 104°   D. 152°

21. Measure to the nearest quarter-inch.
_____

A. $1\frac{1}{4}$in.   B. $1\frac{3}{4}$in.
C. $1\frac{1}{2}$in.   D. 1 in.

22. Measure to the nearest quarter-inch.
_____

A. $1\frac{3}{4}$in.   B. 2 in.
C. $1\frac{1}{2}$in.   D. $2\frac{1}{2}$in.

23. 17 ft = ? yd

A. $5\frac{2}{3}$ B. 51
C. $1\frac{5}{12}$ D. 204

24. 92 in. = ? ft

A. $130\frac{2}{3}$ B. 1104
C. $7\frac{2}{3}$ D. $2\frac{5}{9}$

Semester Test 2, Form A

Name _____

Date _____

Directions: Choose the most reasonable answer. Circle the letter of the answer.

25. The length of a paper clip is about ?	A. 31 mm B. 31 cm C. 31 m D. 31 km
26. A jockey has a mass of about ? kg.	A. 12 B. 100 C. 3000 D. 45
27. Find the area of a rectangle, given $l = 12$ ft and $w = 7$ ft.	A. 19 ft² B. 84 ft² C. 36 ft² D. 42 ft²
28. Find the area of a rectangle, given $l = 21.3$ m and $w = 9.2$ m.	A. 391.92 m² B. 30.5 m² C. 195.96 m² D. 61 m²
29. Find the perimeter of a rectangle, given $l = 25$ cm and $w = 19$ cm.	A. 10,450 cm B. 44 cm C. 20,900 cm D. 88 cm
30. Find the perimeter of a rectangle, given $l = 7\frac{1}{2}$ ft and $w = 3\frac{2}{3}$ ft.	A. $11\frac{1}{6}$ ft B. 165 ft C. $27\frac{1}{2}$ ft D. $22\frac{1}{3}$ ft
31. The area of a rectangle is 368 ft². The width is 16 ft. Find the length.	A. 5888 ft B. 168 ft C. $11\frac{1}{2}$ ft D. 23 ft
32. The area of a rectangle is 49.68 cm². The length is 9.2 cm. Find the width.	A. 15.14 cm B. 447.856 cm C. 5.4 cm D. 115.76 cm

190

Name _____

Date _____

Directions: Choose the most reasonable answer. Circle the letter of the answer.

---

33. The perimeter of a rectangle is 122 mm.
The length is 23 mm. Find the width.

   A. 38 mm   B. 99 mm
   C. 145 mm   D. 290 mm

---

34. The perimeter of a rectangle is 168 in.
The length is 50 in. Find the width.

   A. 118 in.   B. 84 in.
   C. 59 in.   D. 34 in.

---

35. Find the area of a triangle, given
$b = 21$ ft and $h = 8$ ft.

   A. 29 ft²   B. 168 ft²
   C. 84 ft²   D. 13 ft²

---

36. Find the area of a triangle, given
$b = 3.9$ m and $h = 2.4$ m.

   A. 9.36 m²   B. 4.68 m²
   C. 6.3 m²   D. 12.6 m²

---

37. The area of a triangle is 600 yd².
The base is 75 yd. Find the altitude.

   A. 8 yd   B. 16 yd
   C. 32 yd   D. 675 yd

---

38. The area of a triangle is 32.39 m².
The altitude is 7.9 m. Find the base.

   A. 4.1 m   B. 16.4 m
   C. 255.881 m D. 8.2 m

---

39. Find the perimeter of a triangle, given
the the sides measure 10 ft, 21 ft, and 17 ft.

   A. 43 ft   B. 96 ft
   C. 24 ft   D. 48 ft

---

40. Find the perimeter of a triangle, given
that the sides measure 4.0 m, 3.9 m, and 2.5 m.

   A. 10.4 m   B. 20.8 m
   C. 5.2 m   D. 19.5 m

Name _____

Date _____

Directions: Choose the most reasonable answer. Circle the letter of the answer.

41. Find the area of a parallelogram, given $b = 24$ ft and $h = 11$ ft.	A. 132 ft² B. 264 ft² C. 70 ft² D. 140 ft²
42. Find the area of a parallelogram, given $b = 7.2$ m and $h = 5$ m.	A. 36 m² B. 72 m² C. 18 m² D. 24.4 m²
43. Find the perimeter of a parallelogram, given that the measures of two sides are 59 ft and 23 ft.	A. 41 ft B. 82 ft C. 164 ft D. 1357 ft
44. Find the perimeter of a parallelogram, given that the measures of two sides are 8.3 m and 7.9 m.	A. 16.2 m B. 32.4 m C. 76.36 m D. 8.1 m
45. Find the area of a trapezoid, given $b_1 = 7$ in., $b_2 = 13$ in., and $h = 4$ in. where b_1 and b_2 represent the bases.	A. 80 in.² B. 40 in.² C. 364 in.² D. 24 in.²
46. Find the area of a trapezoid, given $b_1 = 1.3$ m, $b_2 = 3.4$ m and $h = 0.8$ m where b_1 and b_2 represent the bases.	A. 0.94 m² B. 3.76 m² C. 1.88 m² D. 5.5 m²
47. Find the perimeter of a trapezoid, given bases $b_1 = 27$ ft, $b_2 = 83$ ft and the other sides measure 61 ft and 75 ft.	A. 123 ft B. 246 ft C. 492 ft D. None of these
48. Find the perimeter of a trapezoid, given bases $b_1 = 43$ cm, $b_2 = 64$ cm, and the other sides measure 15 cm and 13 cm.	A. 67.5 cm B. 270 cm C. 135 cm D. None of these

Name _____

Date _____

Directions: Choose the most reasonable answer. Circle the letter of the answer.

49. Find the volume of a cube, given edge $e = 7$ in.	A. 49 in.³ B. 21 in.³ C. 28 in.³ D. 343 in.³
50. Find the volume of a cube, given edge $e = 10$ cm.	A. 100 cm³ B. 1000 cm³ C. 40 cm³ D. 30 cm³
51. Find the surface area of a cube, given edge $e = 13$ ft.	A. 1014 ft² B. 1352 ft² C. 672 ft² D. 312 ft²
52. Find the surface area of a cube, given edge $e = 7.1$ m.	A. 28.4 m² B. 302.46 m² C. 201.64 m² D. 403.28 m²
53. Find the volume of a rectangular prism, given $l = 4.1$ cm, $w = 3.2$ cm and $h = 1.5$ cm.	A. 17.6 cm³ B. 8.8 cm³ C. 39.36 cm³ D. 19.68 cm³
54. Find the volume of a rectangular prism, given $l = 8$ ft, $w = 3$ ft, and $h = 7$ ft.	A. 84 ft³ B. 18 ft³ C. 168 ft³ D. 336 ft³
55. Find the surface area of a rectangular prism, given $l = 17$ ft, $w = 8$ ft, and $h = 12$ ft.	A. 436 ft² B. 872 ft² C. 340 ft² D. 300 ft²
56. Find the surface area of a rectangular prism, given $l = 36$ mm, $w = 19$ mm and $h = 6$ mm.	A. 1014 mm² B. 900 mm² C. 61 mm² D. 2028 mm²

Name _____

Date _____

Directions: Choose the most reasonable answer. Circle the letter of the answer.

57. The base of a triangular prism has base $b = 15$ in. and altitude $a = 10$ in. Find the volume, if the height of the prism is 38 in.	A. 2850 in.³ B. 5700 in.³ C. 1425 in.³ D. None of these
58. The base of a triangular prism has base $b = 7$ cm and altitude $a = 4$ cm. Find the volume, if the height of the prism is 9.3 cm.	A. 260.4 cm³ B. 130.2 cm³ C. 65.1 cm³ D. 23.3 cm³
59. The triangular base of a pyramid has base $b = 17$ in. and altitude $a = 8$ in. Find the volume, given the height of the pyramid is 9 in.	A. 408 in.³ B. 204 in.³ C. 1224 in.³ D. 225 in.³
60. The triangular base of a pyramid has base $b = 3.5$ cm and altitude $a = 2.4$ cm. Find the volume, given the height of a pyramid is 4.6 cm.	A. 19.32 cm³ B. 38,164 cm³ C. 12.88 cm³ D. 6.44 cm³
61. Find the circumference of a circle, given $r = 29$ cm. Use 3.14 for π.	A. 2640.74 cm B. 91.06 cm C. 32.14 cm D. 182.12 cm
62. Find the circumference of a circle, given $d = 14$ ft. Use $\frac{22}{7}$ for π.	A. 88 ft B. 44 ft C. 154 ft D. 308 ft
63. Find the area of a circle, given $r = 3.5$ m. Use 3.14 for π.	A. 43.96 m² B. 21.98 m² C. 10.99 m² D. 38.465 m²
64. Find the area of a circle, given $d = 42$ in. Use $\frac{22}{7}$ for π.	A. 132 in.² B. 1386 in.² C. 5544 in.² D. None of these

Name _____

Date _____

Directions: Choose the most reasonable answer. Circle the letter of the answer.

---

65. Find the volume of a cylinder, given
$r = 9$ cm and $h = 2$ cm. Use 3.14 for π.

   A. 508.68 cm³   B. 2034.72 cm³

   C. 56.62 cm³   D. 21.14 cm³

---

66. Find the volume of a cylinder, given
$r = 34$ in. and $h = 10$ in. Use $\frac{22}{7}$ for π.

   A. 15,400 in.³   B. 2200 in.³

   C. 38,500 in.³   D. 7700 in.³

---

67. Find the surface area of a cylinder, given
$r = 12$ cm and $h = 9$ cm. Use 3.14 for π.

   A. 1582.56 cm²   B. 339.12 cm²

   C. 84.36 cm²   D. 169.56 cm²

---

68. Find the surface area of a cylinder, given
$r = 7$ in. and $h = 3$ in. Use $\frac{22}{7}$ for π.

   A. 880 in.²   B. 1100 in.²

   C. 440 in.²   D. 70 in.²

---

69. Find the volume of a cone, given
$r = 28$ in. and $h = 12$ in. Use $\frac{22}{7}$ for π.

   A. 1056 in.³   B. 9856 in.³

   C. 29,568 in.³   D. 2464 in.³

---

70. Find the volume of a cone, given
$r = 8$ cm and $h = 15$ cm. Use 3.14 for π.

   A. 125.6 cm³   B. 3014.4 cm³

   C. 1004.8 cm³   D. 376.8 cm³

---

71. Find the volume of a sphere, given
$r = 6$ cm. Use 3.14 for π.

   A. 678.24 cm³   B. 904.32 cm³

   C. 150.72 cm³   D. 226.08 cm³

---

72. Find the volume of a sphere, given
$r = 3\frac{1}{2}$ in. Use $\frac{22}{7}$ for π.

   A. $179\frac{2}{3}$ in.³   B. $269\frac{1}{2}$ in.³

   C. $44\frac{11}{12}$ in.³   D. None of these

Name _____

Date _____

Directions: Choose the most reasonable answer. Circle the letter of the answer.

73. Complete, by following the pattern. 1, 3, 6, 10, —, —, —, —, —, —.	A. 15, 21, 28, 36, 45, 55 B. 12, 14, 16, 18, 20, 22 C. 13, 16, 19, 21, 24, 27 D. None of these
74. Complete, by following the pattern. 0, 3, 8, 15, —, —, —, —, —, —.	A. 30, 60, 120, 240, 480, 960 B. 24, 35, 48, 63, 80, 99 C. 20, 25, 30, 35, 40, 45 D. None of these
75. Complete, by following the pattern. 1, 1, 2, 3, 5, —, —, —, —, —, —.	A. 6, 7, 8, 9, 10, 11 B. 5, 7, 9, 11, 13, 15 C. 8, 13, 21, 34, 55, 89 D. None of these
76. Find the average of 43, 57, and 92.	A. 48 B. 96 C. 192 D. 64
77. Find the average of 132, 341, 627, 243, and 417.	A. 440 B. 176 C. 880 D. 352
78. Find the average of 384, 274, 801, and 673.	A. $266\frac{1}{2}$ B. 1066 C. 436 D. 533
79. Find the exact square root of 841.	A. 5.099 B. 5.385 C. 26 D. 29
80. Find the approximate square root of 24.	A. 625 B. 576 C. 4.899 D. 4.583

Directions: Choose the most reasonable answer. Circle the letter of the answer.

81. What was the total amount spent for gas and electricity for the first six months of the year?

A. $331   B. $362

C. $344   D. $250

82. What was the total amount spent for gas and electricity for the last six months of the year?

A. $344   B. $209

C. $276   D. $300

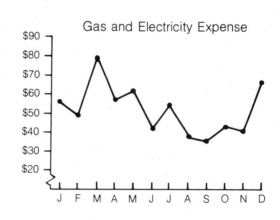

Gas and Electricity Expense

83. What is the total average monthly rainfall for June, July, August, and September?

A. 22.5 in.   B. 19.5 in.

C. 15.5 in.   D. 18 in.

84. What is the total average monthly rainfall for January, February, March, and April?

A. 17.1 in.   B. 25.2 in.

C. 171 in.   D. 8.5 in.

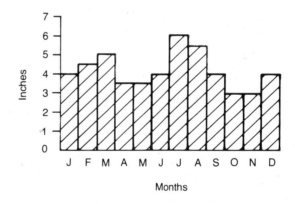

Georgia's Average Monthly Rainfall

85. If there were 84 points for quizzes, how many points were there for tests?

A. 231   B. 462

C. 700   D. 550

86. If there were 715 points for tests, how many points were there for quizzes?

A. 400   B. 130

C. 550   D. 260

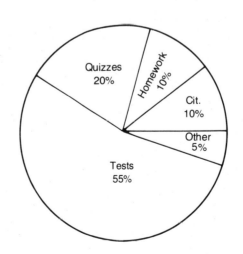

Name _____

Date _____

Directions: Choose the most reasonable answer. Circle the letter of the answer.

87. A purchase of $6.72 is taken from $20. What is the most efficient change?

	$10	$5	$1	50¢	25¢	10¢	5¢	1¢
A.	1		3			2	1	3
B.	1		3		1			3
C.		1		1		2		2
D.			13			2	1	3

88. A purchase of $11.57 is taken from $20. What is the most efficient change?

	$10	$5	$1	50¢	25¢	10¢	5¢	1¢
A.		1	3		1	1	1	3
B.		8			1	1	1	3
C.		1	3			4		3
D.		1	3				8	3

89. Which is the best buy?

A. 64 oz for $1.28   B. 13 oz for 27¢

C. 20 oz for 46¢   D. 32 oz for 61¢

90. Which is the best buy?

A. 65 kg for $1.99   B. 40 kg for $1.35

C. 124 kg for $4.19   D. 354 kg for $11.95

91. Anne worked 7 hr 50 min on Monday, 5 hr 20 min on Tuesday, 3 hr 15 min on Wednesday, 6 hr 12 min on Thursday, and 9 hr 35 min on Friday. What was the total time worked?

A. 31 hr 32 min   B. 30 hr 12 min

C. 32 hr 12 min   D. 27 hr 19 min

92. Find the annual interest earned on $1500 invested at 13% per year.

A. $115.38   B. $19.50

C. $1.95   D. $195.00

Name _____

Date _____

Directions: Choose the most reasonable answer. Circle the letter of the answer.

---

93. The Lopez family had the following food bills for five months: $276.92, $225.13, $314.16, $205.10, and $245.09. What was the average monthly food cost?

A. $316.60   B. $253.28

C. $633.20   D. $1266.40

---

94. Ricardo drove 3420 miles on 152 gallons of fuel. How many miles per gallon did he average?

A. 15.1   B. 19.2

C. 22.5   D. 30.6

---

95. A suit is purchased for $85. The suit is sold at a profit of 17%. Find the selling price.

A. $70.55   B. $14.45

C. $90.00   D. $99.45

---

96. The Firecracker Express traveled 2352 miles at an average of 49 miles per hour. How many hours did the trip take?

A. 112,896   B. 115,248

C. 48   D. 2401

---

97. Mr. Manycattle earns $15.92 an hour. What is his gross pay for 48 hours of work?

A. $76.42   B. $7641.60

C. $764.16   D. None of these

---

98. Leora had a balance of $315.27 in her checking account. Then she wrote a check for $28.57. What was her balance then?

A. $286.70   B. $343.84

C. $287.70   D. $342.84

---

99. A classroom in the shape of a rectangle is 20 ft by 24 ft. How many one-foot square tiles will it take to cover the floor?

A. 88   B. 480

C. 960   D. 166

---

100. Eric bought a suit for $165.00 at a 40% off sale. What was the original price of the suit?

A. $275.00   B. $231.00

C. $412.50   D. $264.00

Name _____

Date _____

Directions: Choose the most reasonable answer. Circle the letter of the answer.

1. Measure to the nearest millimeter. _____	A. 2.3 mm B. 3.2 mm C. 23 mm D. 32 mm
2. Measure to the nearest tenth-centimeter. _____	A. 0.067 cm B. 67.0 cm C. 6.7 cm D. 670.0 cm
3. 14 km = ? m	A. 1.4 B. 14,000 C. 140 D. 1400
4. 2.8 m = ? cm	A. 0.028 B. 0.28 C. 2800 D. 280
5. 142 cm = ? mm	A. 1.42 B. 14.2 C. 1420 D. 14,200
6. 95 mm = ? m	A. 0.095 B. 950 C. 95,000 D. 9.5
7. 520 min = ? hr	A. $8\frac{2}{3}$ B. 31,200 C. $83\frac{2}{3}$ D. $\frac{13}{90}$
8. 77 weeks = ? days	A. 539 B. 11 C. 308 D. $19\frac{1}{4}$

Name _____

Date _____

Directions: Choose the most reasonable answer. Circle the letter of the answer.

---

9. Add.

5 hr   48 min
7 hr   55 min

A. 12 hr 43 min   B. 13 hr 43 min

C. 13 hr 3 min   D. 12 hr 3 min

---

10. Add.

8 mo   4 wk   27 days
7 mo   9 wk   36 days

A. 20 mo 2 wk   B. 15 mo 2 wk

C. 18 mo 1 wk   D. 19 mo 2 wk

---

11. Subtract.

34 hr   15 min
18 hr   37 min

A. 15 hr 22 min   B. 15 hr 38 min

C. 15 hr 78 min   D. 15 hr 18 min

---

12. Subtract.

17 yr   2 mo   3 wk
12 yr   9 mo   5 wk

A. 4 yr 4 mo 2 wk   B. 16 yr 2 wk

C. 16 yr 2 mo 2 wk   D. 3 yr 2 mo 2 wk

---

13. 75°C = ? °F

A. 157   B. $23\frac{8}{9}$

C. 167   D. 192.6

---

14. 86°F = ? °C

A. $65\frac{5}{9}$ B. $15\frac{5}{9}$

C. $77\frac{7}{9}$ D. 30

---

15. Find the measure of ∠A.

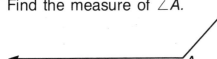

A. 43°   B. 137°

C. 47°   D. 143°

---

16. Find the measure of ∠B.

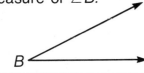

A. 64°   B. 154°

C. 26°   D. 34°

Name _____

Date _____

Directions: Choose the most reasonable answer. Circle the letter of the answer.

17. $\angle C$ and $\angle D$ are complementary angles. $\angle C$ measures 32°. Find the measure of $\angle D$.	A. 122° B. 148° C. 58° D. 68°
18. $\angle E$ and $\angle F$ are complementary angles. $\angle E$ measures 71°. Find the measure of $\angle F$.	A. 109° B. 19° C. 29° D. 42°
19. $\angle G$ and $\angle H$ are supplementary angles. $\angle G$ measures 67°. Find the measure of $\angle H$.	A. 23° B. 113° C. 33° D. 143°
20. $\angle J$ and $\angle K$ are supplementary angles. $\angle J$ measures 42°. Find the measure of $\angle K$.	A. 138° B. 58° C. 48° D. 118°
21. Measure to the nearest quarter-inch. _____	A. 2 in. B. $2\frac{1}{4}$in. C. $2\frac{1}{2}$in. D. $1\frac{3}{4}$in.
22. Measure to the nearest quarter-inch. _____	A. $\frac{3}{4}$in. B. $\frac{1}{2}$in. C. 1 in. D. $1\frac{1}{2}$in.
23. 58 yd = ? ft	A. $4\frac{5}{6}$ B. $19\frac{1}{3}$ C. 174 D. 696
24. 47 ft = ? in.	A. 564 B. $3\frac{11}{12}$ C. 141 D. $15\frac{2}{3}$

Name _____

Date _____

Directions: Choose the most reasonable answer. Circle the letter of the answer.

---

25. A man is about ? tall.

    A. 2 m   B. 2 km

    C. 2 cm   D. 2 mm

---

26. A liter of milk has a mass of about ? g.

    A. 100   B. 1000

    C. 10   D. 1

---

27. Find the area of a rectangle, given
$l = 14$ ft and $w = 12$ ft.

    A. 26 ft²   B. 84 ft²

    C. 52 ft²   D. 168 ft²

---

28. Find the area of a rectangle, given
$l = 47.2$ cm and $w = 21.2$ cm.

    A. 500.32 cm²   B. 68.4 cm²

    C. 1000.64 cm²   D. 136.8 cm²

---

29. Find the perimeter of a rectangle, given
$l = 14$ m and $w = 9$ m.

    A. 23 m   B. 126 m

    C. 46 m   D. 63 m

---

30. Find the perimeter of a rectangle, given
$l = 9\frac{2}{3}$ ft and $w = 5\frac{1}{4}$ ft.

    A. $24\frac{7}{12}$ ft   B. $101\frac{1}{2}$ ft

    C. $14\frac{11}{12}$ ft   D. $29\frac{5}{6}$ ft

---

31. The area of a rectangle is 714 ft².
The width is 17 ft. Find the length.

    A. 42 ft   B. 340 ft

    C. 697 ft   D. 680 ft

---

32. The area of a rectangle is 156.18 cm².
The length is 13.7 cm. Find the width.

    A. 142.48 cm   B. 11.4 cm

    C. 64.39 cm   D. 128.78 cm

Name _____

Date _____

Directions: Choose the most reasonable answer. Circle the letter of the answer.

33. The perimeter of a rectangle is 156 cm. The length is 48 cm. Find the width.	A. 7488 cm B. 30 cm C. 3.25 cm D. 108 cm
34. The perimeter of a rectangle is 204 ft. The length is 72 ft. Find the width.	A. 30 ft B. $2\frac{5}{6}$ ft C. 132 ft D. 14,688 ft
35. Find the area of a triangle, given $b = 35$ ft and $h = 20$ ft.	A. 700 ft² B. 350 ft² C. 110 ft² D. 55 ft²
36. Find the area of a triangle, given $b = 8.2$ m and $h = 12.4$ m.	A. 101.68 m² B. 25.42 m² C. 50.84 m² D. 41.2 m²
37. The area of a triangle is 189 ft². The base is 27 ft. Find the altitude.	A. 28 ft B. 7 ft C. 14 ft D. 162 ft
38. The area of a triangle is 586.16 cm². The altitude is 27.2 cm. Find the base.	A. 86.2 cm B. 21.55 cm C. 43.1 cm D. 265.88 cm
39. Find the perimeter of a triangle, given that the sides measure 27 in., 36 in., and 46 in.	A. 109 in. B. $54\frac{1}{2}$ in. C. 218 in. D. 136 in.
40. Find the perimeter of a triangle, given that the sides measure 72 cm, 81 cm, and 97 cm.	A. 250 cm B. 125 cm C. 500 cm D. 322 cm

Name _____

Date _____

Directions: Choose the most reasonable answer. Circle the letter of the answer.

---

41. Find the area of a parallelogram, given
$b = 7.5$ m and $h = 3.7$ m.

    A. 22.4 m²   B. 55.5 m²
    C. 13.87 m²   D. 27.75 m²

---

42. Find the area of a parallelogram, given
$b = 63$ in. and $h = 24$ in.

    A. 174 in.²   B. 378 in.²
    C. 756 in.²   D. 1512 in.²

---

43. Find the perimeter of a parallelogram, given
that the measures of two sides are 62 cm
and 94 cm.

    A. 2914 cm   B. 5828 cm
    C. 156 cm   D. 312 cm

---

44. Find the perimeter of a parallelogram, given
that the measures of two sides are 12.6 m
and 15.9 m.

    A. 114 m   B. 57 m
    C. 28.5 m   D. 14.25 m

---

45. Find the area of a trapezoid, given
$b_1 = 12$ m, $b_2 = 7$ m, and $h = 6$ m
where b_1 and b_2 represent the bases.

    A. 25 m²   B. 114 m²
    C. 66 m²   D. 57 m²

---

46. Find the area of a trapezoid, given
$b_1 = 36$ in., $b_2 = 48$ in., and $h = 21$ in.
where b_1 and b_2 represent the bases.

    A. 1764 in.²   B. 882 in.²
    C. 441 in.²   D. 1044 in.²

---

47. Find the perimeter of a trapezoid, given
bases $b_1 = 32$ yd, $b_2 = 29$ yd, and the
other sides measure 24 yd and 17 yd.

    A. 469 yd   B. 204 yd
    C. 51 yd   D. 102 yd

---

48. Find the perimeter of a trapezoid, given
bases $b_1 = 48$ cm, $b_2 = 81$ cm, and the
other sides measure 63 cm and 51 cm.

    A. 486 cm   B. 243 cm
    C. 121.5 cm   D. 3342 cm

Semester Test 2, Form B

Name _____

Date _____

Directions: Choose the most reasonable answer. Circle the letter of the answer.

---

49. Find the volume of a cube, given edge $e = 5$ cm.

A. 30 cm³ B. 15 cm³
C. 125 cm³ D. 20 cm³

---

50. Find the volume of a cube, given edge $e = 14$ in.

A. 2744 in.³ B. 56 in.³
C. 84 in.³ D. 42 in.³

---

51. Find the surface area of a cube, given edge $e = 25$ ft.

A. 100 ft² B. 2500 ft²
C. 150 ft² D. 3750 ft²

---

52. Find the surface area of a cube, given edge $e = 12.2$ cm.

A. 595.36 cm² B. 148.84 cm²
C. 73.2 cm² D. 893.04 cm²

---

53. Find the volume of a rectangular prism, given $l = 8\frac{1}{2}$ ft, $w = 4$ ft, and $h = 2\frac{1}{4}$ ft.

A. $76\frac{1}{2}$ ft³ B. 153 ft³
C. $14\frac{3}{4}$ ft³ D. $71\frac{1}{2}$ ft³

---

54. Find the volume of a rectangular prism, given $l = 7.3$ m, $w = 8.1$ m, and $h = 5.7$ m.

A. 674.082 m³ B. 337.041 m³
C. 53.47 m³ D. 42.2 m³

---

55. Find the surface area of a rectangular prism, given $l = 24$ ft, $w = 17$ ft, and $h = 12$ ft.

A. 900 ft² B. 492 ft²
C. 1800 ft² D. 612 ft²

---

56. Find the surface area of a rectangular prism, given $l = 25$ cm, $w = 19$ cm and $h = 13$ cm.

A. 1522 cm² B. 1275 cm²
C. 1047 cm² D. 2094 cm²

Name _____

Date _____

Directions: Choose the most reasonable answer. Circle the letter of the answer.

57. The base of a triangular prism has base $b = 25$ in. and altitude $a = 13$ in. Find the volume, if the height of the prism is 22 in.	A. 7150 in.³ C. 3575 in.³	B. 836 in.³ D. $1191\frac{2}{3}$ in.³
58. The base of a triangular prism has base $b = 2.3$ cm and altitude $a = 3.1$ cm. Find the volume, if the height of the prism is 1.4 cm.	A. 9.982 cm³ C. 7.56 cm³	B. 4.991 cm³ D. 1.66 cm³
59. The triangular base of a pyramid has base $b = 27$ in. and altitude $a = 12$ in. Find the volume, given the height of the pyramid is 13 in.	A. 702 in.³ C. 6318 in.³	B. 2106 in.³ D. 4212 in.³
60. The triangular base of a pyramid has base $b = 18$ cm and altitude $a = 11$ cm. Find the volume, given the height of a pyramid is 5.1 cm.	A. 504.9 cm³ C. 336.6 cm³	B. 1009.1 cm³ D. 168.3 cm³
61. Find the circumference of a circle, given $r = 15$ cm. Use 3.14 for π.	A. 94.2 cm C. 47.1 cm	B. 706.5 cm D. 1413 cm
62. Find the circumference of a circle, given $d = 21$ ft. Use $\frac{22}{7}$ for π.	A. 66 ft C. 33 ft	B. 1386 ft D. 346.5 ft
63. Find the area of a circle, given $r = 3\frac{1}{2}$ ft. Use $\frac{22}{7}$ for π.	A. $19\frac{1}{4}$ ft² C. 308 ft²	B. 154 ft² D. $38\frac{1}{2}$ ft²
64. Find the area of a circle, given $r = 2.5$ m. Use 3.14 for π.	A. 19.625 m² C. 6.25 m²	B. 7.85 m² D. 15.7 m²

Name _____

Date _____

Directions: Choose the most reasonable answer. Circle the letter of the answer.

65. Find the volume of a cylinder, given $r = 8$ cm and $h = 5$ cm. Use 3.14 for π.	A. 125.6 cm³ B. 1004.8 cm³ C. 630 cm³ D. 502.4 cm³
66. Find the volume of a cylinder, given $r = 28$ in. and $h = 10$ in. Use $\frac{22}{7}$ for π.	A. 12,320 in.³ B. 2464 in.³ C. 24,640 in.³ D. 880 in.³
67. Find the surface area of a cylinder, given $r = 9.5$ cm and $h = 6$ cm. Use 3.14 for π.	A. 357.96 cm² B. 178.98 cm² C. 1700.31 cm² D. 924.73 cm²
68. Find the surface area of a cylinder, given $r = 16$ in. and $h = 19$ in. Use $\frac{22}{7}$ for π.	A. 28,160 in.² B. 1760 in.² C. 3520 in.² D. 14,030 in.²
69. Find the volume of a cone, given $r = 12$ in. and $h = 14$ in. Use $\frac{22}{7}$ for π.	A. 6336 in.³ B. 2112 in.³ C. 1006 in.³ D. 2464 in.³
70. Find the volume of a cone, given $r = 15$ cm and $h = 13$ cm. Use 3.14 for π.	A. 2653.3 cm³ B. 9184.5 cm³ C. 3061.5 cm³ D. 204.1 cm³
71. Find the volume of a sphere, given $r = 3$ m. Use 3.14 for π.	A. 339.12 m³ B. 113.04 m³ C. 37.68 m³ D. 84.78 cm³
72. Find the volume of a sphere, given $r = 9$ ft. Use 3.14 for π.	A. 9156.24 ft³ B. 28.26 ft³ C. 3052.08 ft³ D. 254.34 ft³

Name _____

Date _____

Directions: Choose the most reasonable answer. Circle the letter of the answer.

73. Complete, by following the pattern. 5, 6, 10, 19, —, —, —, —, —, —.	A. 28, 37, 46, 55, 64, 73 B. 35, 60, 96, 145, 209, 290 C. 11, 12, 13, 14, 15, 16 D. None of these
74. Complete, by following the pattern. 2, 5, 10, 17, —, —, —, —, —, —.	A. 22, 27, 32, 37, 42, 47 B. 24, 31, 38, 45, 52, 59 C. 26, 37, 50, 65, 82, 101 D. None of these
75. Complete, by following the pattern. 3, 9, 19, 33, —, —, —, —, —, —.	A. 51, 73, 99, 129, 163, 201 B. 43, 53, 63, 73, 83, 93 C. 47, 61, 75, 89, 103, 127 D. None of these
76. Find the average of 63, 72, and 96.	A. 462 B. 231 C. $115\frac{1}{2}$ D. 77
77. Find the average of 164, 341, 265, 506, and 234.	A. 755 B. 302 C. 151 D. 1510
78. Find the average of 523, 635, 432, and 714.	A. 2304 B. 1152 C. 288 D. 576
79. Find the exact square root of 1369.	A. 6.164 B. 6.083 C. 43 D. 37
80. Find the approximate square root of 51.	A. 2601 B. 7.681 C. 7.141 D. 3481

Semester Test 2, Form B

Name _____

Date _____

Directions: Choose the most reasonable answer. Circle the letter of the answer.

81. Which country has the greatest difference between birth rate and death rate?

A. Mexico   B. United Kingdom

C. France   D. India

82. Which country has the least difference between birth rate and death rate?

A. Mexico   B. United Kingdom

C. France   D. India

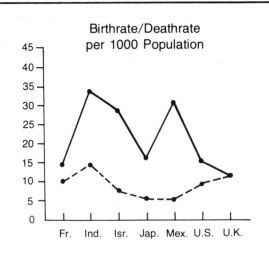

Birthrate/Deathrate per 1000 Population

Fr. Ind. Isr. Jap. Mex. U.S. U.K.

83. What percent of the budget is spent for food, clothing, and shelter combined?

A. 50%   B. 33%

C. 39%   D. 100%

84. What percent of the budget is spent for utilities, personal care, and transportation combined?

A. 100%   B. 50%

C. 21%   D. 25%

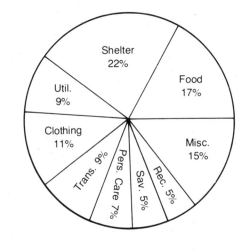

Shelter 22%
Food 17%
Util. 9%
Misc. 15%
Clothing 11%
Trans. 9%
Pers. Care 7%
Sav. 5%
Rec. 5%

85. Which city has population between 3 and 4 million?

A. New York   B. Los Angeles

C. Chicago   D. Houston

86. Which city has population between 2 and 3 million?

A. Chicago   B. New York

C. Los Angeles   D. Houston

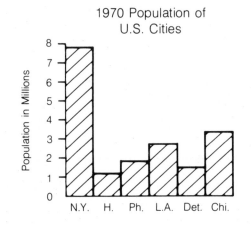

1970 Population of U.S. Cities

Population in Millions

N.Y. H. Ph. L.A. Det. Chi.

Name _____

Date _____

Directions: Choose the most reasonable answer. Circle the letter of the answer.

87. A purchase of $7.81 is taken from $20. What is the most efficient change?		$10	$5	$1	50¢	25¢	10¢	5¢	1¢
	A.	1		2	1		3		1
	B.			12				3	4
	C.	1		2	1	1		1	1
	D.	1		2			1	1	4

88. A purchase of $13.87 is taken from $20. What is the most efficient change?		$10	$5	$1	50¢	25¢	10¢	5¢	1¢
	A.		1	1				2	3
	B.		1	1			1		3
	C.	1		3	1	1	1		2
	D.	1		3			8		2

89. Which is the best buy?

   A. 102 oz for $3.25   B. 16 oz for $0.56

   C. 64 oz for $2.05   D. 32 oz for $0.99

90. Which is the best buy?

   A. 325 kg for $8.12   B. 200 kg for $5.40

   C. 250 kg for $7.75   D. 400 kg for $10.80

91. Anne worked 5 hr 20 min on Monday, 7 hr 55 min on Tuesday, 3 hr 27 min on Wednesday, 8 hr 43 min on Thursday, and 7 hr 45 min on Friday. What was the total time she worked?

   A. 33 hr 10 min   B. 30 hr 10 min

   C. 30 hr   D. 33 hr

92. Find the annual interest earned on $1750 invested at 12% per year.

   A. $105   B. $21,000

   C. $21   D. $210

Directions: Choose the most reasonable answer. Circle the letter of the answer.

93. Juanita made grades of 95, 84, 73, 87, 79, and 92 on six tests. What was the average grade?	A. 87 B. 85 C. 73 D. 83
94. Hamilton took 19 hours to drive 741 miles. What was his average rate for the trip?	A. 14,079 mph B. 39 mph C. 57 mph D. None of these
95. A dressed marked $49.50 is on sale for 30% off. What is the sale price?	A. $84.15 B. $14.85 C. $64.35 D. $34.65
96. A dealer sold 25 new cars for a total of $180,725. What was the average price of each?	A. $90,362.50 B. $9036.25 C. $7229 D. None of these
97. Kevin earns $7.50 an hour. What is his net pay if he works 38 hours and has deductions totaling $8.15?	A. $276.85 B. $285.00 C. $293.15 D. $594.70
98. A room measures 27 feet by 45 feet. How many square yards of carpet are required to cover the floor?	A. 45 B. 162 C. 81 D. 135
99. Helen had a balance of $324.42 in her checking account. She deposited checks of $39.51, $48.72, and $112.19. What was her balance after the deposits?	A. $124.00 B. $200.42 C. $524.84 D. None of these
100. A total of 702 students purchased the yearbook. This was 78% of the school enrollment. What was the enrollment?	A. 900 B. 1200 C. 1000 D. None of these

ANSWERS

Page 1   **1.** 31   **2.** 451,841   **3.** 792   **4.** 1043   **5.** 200   **6.** 159   **7.** 1290   **8.** 1435   **9.** 7,019,491   **10.** 12,505   **11.** 28,813   **12.** 53,605,943   **13.** 407,697   **14.** 293,672   **15.** 891

Page 2   **1.** 31   **2.** 684,832   **3.** 925   **4.** 1115   **5.** 260   **6.** 146   **7.** 1223   **8.** 1645   **9.** 717,040   **10.** 13,581   **11.** 38,826   **12.** 50,712,022   **13.** 507,507   **14.** 380,034   **15.** 1005

Page 3   **1.** 32   **2.** 633,801   **3.** 819   **4.** 608   **5.** 335   **6.** 201   **7.** 1776   **8.** 1417   **9.** 825,882   **10.** 11,449   **11.** 44,637   **12.** 78,645,522   **13.** 807,974   **14.** 675,414   **15.** 1228

Page 4   **1.** 30   **2.** 443,535   **3.** 894   **4.** 982   **5.** 215   **6.** 159   **7.** 2063   **8.** 1585   **9.** 8,022,935   **10.** 14,777   **11.** 60,441   **12.** 68,519,514   **13.** 907,369   **14.** 441,398   **15.** 1335

Page 5   **1.** 374   **2.** 401   **3.** 69,407   **4.** 5125   **5.** 7959   **6.** 642   **7.** 559   **8.** 439   **9.** 212   **10.** 3394   **11.** 46,177   **12.** 715,692   **13.** 3565   **14.** 426   **15.** 702,625

Page 6   **1.** 322   **2.** 174   **3.** 46,258   **4.** 589   **5.** 36,682   **6.** 34   **7.** 67   **8.** 199   **9.** 278   **10.** 69,072   **11.** 83,953   **12.** 454,849   **13.** 304   **14.** 1962   **15.** 539,432

Page 7   **1.** 81,171   **2.** 1110   **3.** 6038   **4.** 15,142   **5.** 15,969   **6.** 473   **7.** 8859   **8.** 65,821   **9.** 1909   **10.** 5556   **11.** 5521   **12.** 8788   **13.** 51   **14.** 5889   **15.** 46,779

Page 8   **1.** 60,919   **2.** 9005   **3.** 65,813   **4.** 25,883   **5.** 17,877   **6.** 499   **7.** 21,819   **8.** 5244   **9.** 2907   **10.** 23,587   **11.** 22,096   **12.** 29,091   **13.** 201   **14.** 17,509   **15.** 56,068

Page 9   **1.** 84   **2.** 2736   **3.** 3132   **4.** 1788   **5.** 4215   **6.** 8376   **7.** 696   **8.** 4617   **9.** 4192   **10.** 2034   **11.** 1612   **12.** 589

Page 10   **1.** 45   **2.** 120   **3.** 108   **4.** 252   **5.** 376   **6.** 261   **7.** 2217   **8.** 5283   **9.** 828   **10.** 2985   **11.** 5901   **12.** 11,488

Page 11   **1.** 102   **2.** 160   **3.** 29   **4.** 324   **5.** 294   **6.** 180   **7.** 80   **8.** 243   **9.** 294   **10.** 1377   **11.** 2136   **12.** 2436

Page 12   **1.** 27   **2.** 392   **3.** 345   **4.** 140   **5.** 324   **6.** 280   **7.** 105   **8.** 603   **9.** 371   **10.** 7740   **11.** 5139   **12.** 816

Page 13.   **1.** 180   **2.** 840   **3.** 160   **4.** 3948   **5.** 1470   **6.** 3916   **7.** 1290   **8.** 6739   **9.** 26,934   **10.** 12,420   **11.** 27,945   **12.** 75,072

Page 14   **1.** 595   **2.** 720   **3.** 2204   **4.** 3108   **5.** 320   **6.** 1829   **7.** 17,556   **8.** 4108   **9.** 12,410   **10.** 21,567   **11.** 26,880   **12.** 42,164

Page 15   **1.** 1075   **2.** 1120   **3.** 2314   **4.** 741   **5.** 4368   **6.** 520   **7.** 9108   **8.** 32,712   **9.** 5662   **10.** 18,688   **11.** 39,886   **12.** 4410

Page 16   **1.** 940   **2.** 468   **3.** 900   **4.** 884   **5.** 6975   **6.** 1230   **7.** 33,990   **8.** 37,656   **9.** 68,262   **10.** 15,360   **11.** 21,112   **12.** 26,625

Page 17   **1.** 24,345   **2.** 3572   **3.** 256,690   **4.** 2106   **5.** 74,601   **6.** 2044   **7.** 1776   **8.** 12,193   **9.** 0   **10.** 684   **11.** 842,062,238   **12.** 391

Page 18   **1.** 93,852   **2.** 4464   **3.** 4,059,594   **4.** 1836   **5.** 76,912   **6.** 3293   **7.** 4752   **8.** 33,166,457   **9.** 1083   **10.** 375   **11.** 1564   **12.** 168

Page 19   **1.** 59,056   **2.** 2241   **3.** 263,835   **4.** 2331   **5.** 83,842   **6.** 1918   **7.** 4515   **8.** 9116   **9.** 0   **10.** 385   **11.** 2,960,171,360   **12.** 384

Page 20   **1.** 55,376   **1.** 546   **3.** 375,669   **4.** 2183   **5.** 421,902   **6.** 4232   **7.** 1428   **8.** 101,565   **9.** 0   **10.** 3416   **11.** 4,986,044,850   **12.** 756

Page 21   **1.** 9   **2.** 6   **3.** 7   **4.** 0   **5.** 8   **6.** 8   **7.** 9   **8.** 8   **9.** 7   **10.** 5   **11.** 3   **12.** 7   **13.** 10   **14.** 8   **15.** 9   **16.** 5   **17.** 4   **18.** 5   **19.** 3   **20.** 6   **21.** 10   **22.** 4   **23.** 6   **24.** 4   **25.** 8   **26.** 6   **27.** 7   **28.** 5   **29.** 0   **30.** 2

Page 22   **1.** 8 r 2   **2.** 8 r 1   **3.** 7 r 1   **4.** 8 r 2   **5.** 0 r 1   **6.** 7 r 3   **7.** 5 r 3   **8.** 6 r 2   **9.** 4 r 1   **10.** 6 r 6   **11.** 6 r 2   **12.** 6 r 3   **13.** 4 r 7   **14.** 6 r 3   **15.** 6 r 1   **16.** 8 r 2   **17.** 9 r 2   **18.** 9 r 2   **19.** 7 r 5   **20.** 7 r 5   **21.** 5 r 2   **22.** 8 r 3   **23.** 4 r 3   **24.** 7 r 5   **25.** 8 r 2   **26.** 8 r 1   **27.** 6 r 1   **28.** 3 r 3   **29.** 8 r 3   **30.** 9 r 1

Page 23   **1.** 3 r 1   **2.** 2 r 2   **3.** 7 r 1   **4.** 6 r 3   **5.** 7 r 1   **6.** 4 r 4   **7.** 6 r 1   **8.** 5 r 4   **9.** 6 r 3   **10.** 7 r 3   **11.** 6 r 3   **12.** 7 r 3   **13.** 7 r 2   **14.** 6 r 7   **15.** 7 r 1   **16.** 4 r 6   **17.** 3 r 2   **18.** 5 r 1   **19.** 4 r 4   **20.** 7 r 2   **21.** 4 r 3   **22.** 6 r 6   **23.** 3 r 5   **24.** 2 r 3   **25.** 8 r 1   **26.** 7 r 5   **27.** 8 r 1   **28.** 7 r 1   **29.** 3 r 2   **30.** 9 r 2

Page 24   **1.** 9 r 3   **2.** 6 r 6   **3.** 4 r 3   **4.** 5 r 6   **5.** 8 r 1   **6.** 8 r 1   **7.** 3 r 6   **8.** 5 r 4   **9.** 5 r 7   **10.** 3 r 4   **11.** 4 r 7   **12.** 8 r 2   **13.** 6 r 1   **14.** 6 r 2   **15.** 5 r 1   **16.** 3 r 1   **17.** 2 r 4   **18.** 6 r 2   **19.** 4 r 1   **20.** 2 r 6   **21.** 5 r 1   **22.** 3 r 2   **23.** 5 r 2   **24.** 3 r 1   **25.** 8 r 1   **26.** 4 r 2   **27.** 5 r 5   **28.** 5 r 3   **29.** 7 r 4   **30.** 5 r 2

Page 25   **1.** 42   **2.** 19   **3.** 92   **4.** 27   **5.** 61   **6.** 89   **7.** 67   **8.** 91   **9.** 67   **10.** 88   **11.** 31   **12.** 87

Page 26   **1.** 77   **2.** 89   **3.** 23   **4.** 46   **5.** 52   **6.** 71   **7.** 37   **8.** 68   **9.** 27   **10.** 50   **11.** 83   **12.** 49

Page 27   **1.** 67   **2.** 23   **3.** 47   **4.** 36   **5.** 71   **6.** 29   **7.** 79   **8.** 52   **9.** 29   **10.** 57   **11.** 63   **12.** 42

Page 28   **1.** 79   **2.** 81   **3.** 46   **4.** 36   **5.** 24   **6.** 83   **7.** 42   **8.** 95   **9.** 37   **10.** 56   **11.** 63   **12.** 25

Page 29   **1.** 29   **2.** 36   **3.** 72   **4.** 59   **5.** 67   **6.** 43   **7.** 26   **8.** 17   **9.** 58   **10.** 35   **11.** 78   **12.** 67

Page 30   **1.** 23   **2.** 17   **3.** 32   **4.** 41   **5.** 92   **6.** 47   **7.** 32   **8.** 58   **9.** 45   **10.** 52   **11.** 41   **12.** 27

Page 31   **1.** 21   **2.** 48   **3.** 22   **4.** 41   **5.** 32   **6.** 15   **7.** 26   **8.** 52   **9.** 14   **10.** 62   **11.** 27   **12.** 32

Page 32   **1.** 43   **2.** 51   **3.** 49   **4.** 22   **5.** 47   **6.** 33   **7.** 51   **8.** 44   **9.** 32   **10.** 43   **11.** 16   **12.** 21

Page 33   **1.** 61   **2.** 154   **3.** 4   **4.** 48   **5.** 131   **6.** 8   **7.** 70   **8.** 347   **9.** 300   **10.** 7   **11.** 24   **12.** 704

Page 34 1. 99 2. 21 3. 81,039 4. 2 5. 23 6. 6 7. 24 8. 63 9. 100 10. 17 11. 13 12. 321

Page 35 1. 53 2. 169 3. 178 4. 252 5. 26,129 6. 10 7. 41 8. 25 9. 252 10. 31 11. 47 12. 4003

Page 36 1. 23 2. 451 3. 219 4. 65 5. 352 6. 34 7. 546 8. 69 9. 10,101 10. 3 11. 512 12. 46

Page 37 1. 297 2. 1,171,275 3. 2598 4. 417,978 5. 136,889 6. 128,149 7. 2436 8. 220,125 9. 205,927,829 10. 613 11. 564 12. 3005

Page 38 1. 273 2. 1,218,829 3. 2116 4. 757,878 5. 289,889 6. 207,979 7. 3216 8. 333,795 9. 108,322,134 10. 909 11. 217 12. 9044

Page 39 1. 239 2. 1,657,395 3. 2014 4. 728,174 5. 18,888 6. 648,567 7. 1276 8. 222,396 9. 349,727,410 10. 81 11. 414 12. 3005

Page 40 1. 273 2. 1,072,583 3. 2965 4. 609,707 5. 517,729 6. 441,988 7. 3886 8. 127,576 9. 146,627,406 10. 705 11. 317 12. 4006

Page 41 1. 5506 2. 1119 3. 378 4. 6048 5. $2875 6. 1568 7. $5985 8. $4

Page 42 1. 472,410 2. $648 3. 5895 4. $1801 5. $750 6. 4464 7. 16 8. 45

Page 43 1. 2363 2. $1868 3. 68,782 4. 629 5. $405 6. 39,215 7. 38 8. $816

Page 44 1. 617 2. 1,281,247 mi² 3. 10,704 ft 4. $67,875 5. 7680 6. 20,805 7. $11 8. 98

Page 45 1. = 2. ≠ 3. ≠ 4. $x = 80$ 5. $x = 1$ 6. $x = 21$ 7. $x = 44$ 8. $x = 78$ 9. $x = 152$ 10. $x = 184$ 11. $x = 35$ 12. $x = 171$

Page 46 1. ≠ 2. ≠ 3. = 4. $x = 20$ 5. $x = 4$ 6. $x = 7$ 7. $x = 9$ 8. $x = 7$ 9. $x = 3$ 10. $x = 11$ 11. $x = 5$ 12. $x = 12$

Page 47 1. ≠ 2. = 3. = 4. $x = 12$ 5. $x = 24$ 6. $x = 100$ 7. $x = 33$ 8. $x = 12$ 9. $x = 4$ 10. $x = 6$ 11. $x = 9$ 12. $x = 6$

Page 48 1. ≠ 2. ≠ 3. = 4. $x = 80$ 5. $x = 7$ 6. $x = 16$ 7. $x = 4$ 8. $x = 11$ 9. $x = 8$ 10. $x = 8$ 11. $x = 7$ 12. $x = 8$

Page 49 1. $\frac{3}{2}$ or $1\frac{1}{2}$ 2. $\frac{9}{8}$ or $1\frac{1}{8}$ 3. $\frac{3}{2}$ or $1\frac{1}{2}$ 4. $\frac{9}{14}$ 5. $\frac{13}{12}$ or $1\frac{1}{12}$ 6. $\frac{21}{20}$ or $1\frac{1}{20}$ 7. $\frac{17}{30}$ 8. $\frac{25}{24}$ or $1\frac{1}{24}$ 9. $\frac{23}{18}$ or $1\frac{5}{18}$ 10. $\frac{19}{12}$ or $1\frac{7}{12}$ 11. $\frac{17}{15}$ or $1\frac{2}{15}$ 12. $\frac{23}{30}$

Page 50 1. $\frac{9}{14}$ 2. $\frac{11}{10}$ or $1\frac{1}{10}$ 3. $\frac{9}{8}$ or $1\frac{1}{8}$ 4. $\frac{5}{6}$ 5. $\frac{19}{21}$ 6. $\frac{6}{7}$ 7. $\frac{43}{30}$ or $1\frac{13}{30}$ 8. $\frac{17}{20}$ 9. $\frac{11}{12}$ 10. $\frac{19}{20}$ 11. $\frac{16}{15}$ or $1\frac{1}{15}$ 12. $\frac{5}{6}$

Page 51 1. $\frac{11}{12}$ 2. $\frac{19}{20}$ 3. $\frac{37}{30}$ or $1\frac{7}{30}$ 4. $\frac{29}{35}$ 5. $\frac{13}{21}$ 6. $\frac{13}{14}$ 7. $\frac{13}{10}$ or $1\frac{3}{10}$ 8. $\frac{7}{8}$ 9. $\frac{7}{6}$ or $1\frac{1}{6}$ 10. $\frac{29}{20}$ or $1\frac{9}{20}$ 11. $\frac{31}{30}$ or $1\frac{1}{30}$ 12. $\frac{49}{30}$ or $1\frac{19}{30}$

Page 52 1. $\frac{26}{21}$ or $1\frac{5}{21}$ 2. $\frac{41}{35}$ or $1\frac{6}{35}$ 3. $\frac{29}{30}$ 4. $\frac{29}{20}$ 5. $\frac{7}{12}$ 6. $\frac{7}{6}$ or $1\frac{1}{6}$ 7. $\frac{13}{8}$ or $1\frac{5}{8}$ 8. $\frac{7}{10}$ 9. $\frac{13}{14}$ 10. $\frac{19}{20}$ 11. $\frac{11}{30}$ 12. $\frac{17}{15}$ or $1\frac{2}{15}$

Page 53 1. $\frac{5}{8}$ 2. $\frac{1}{6}$ 3. $\frac{2}{15}$ 3. $\frac{17}{24}$ 4. $\frac{5}{24}$ 6. $\frac{2}{15}$ 7. $\frac{23}{48}$ 8. $\frac{13}{60}$ 9. $\frac{5}{21}$ 10. $\frac{11}{24}$ 11. $\frac{1}{12}$ 12. $\frac{9}{64}$

Page 54 1. $\frac{1}{9}$ 2. $\frac{8}{45}$ 3. $\frac{5}{20}$ 4. $\frac{3}{20}$ 5. $\frac{11}{24}$ 6. $\frac{5}{8}$ 7. $\frac{1}{2}$ 8. $\frac{5}{9}$ 9. $\frac{5}{18}$ 10. $\frac{11}{15}$ 11. $\frac{11}{24}$ 12. $\frac{13}{28}$

Page 55 1. $\frac{3}{8}$ 2. $\frac{5}{12}$ 3. $\frac{1}{40}$ 4. $\frac{11}{24}$ 5. $\frac{7}{24}$ 6. $\frac{11}{20}$ 7. $\frac{17}{48}$ 8. $\frac{23}{60}$ 9. $\frac{5}{21}$ 10. $\frac{5}{24}$ 11. $\frac{11}{35}$ 12. $\frac{1}{3}$

Page 56 1. $\frac{9}{64}$ 2. $\frac{17}{24}$ 3. $\frac{19}{24}$ 4. $\frac{29}{35}$ 5. $\frac{37}{48}$ 6. $\frac{1}{3}$ 7. $\frac{16}{21}$ 8. $\frac{19}{30}$ 9. $\frac{5}{28}$ 10. $\frac{7}{45}$ 11. $\frac{53}{75}$ 12. $\frac{1}{6}$

Page 57 1. $\frac{11}{75}$ 2. $\frac{6}{11}$ 3. $\frac{1}{4}$ 4. $\frac{1}{2}$ 5. $\frac{9}{31}$ 6. $\frac{6}{35}$ 7. $\frac{519}{850}$ 8. $\frac{50}{729}$ 9. $\frac{1}{30}$ 10. $\frac{77}{9}$ or $8\frac{5}{9}$ 11. $\frac{5}{26}$ 12. $\frac{1}{11}$

Page 58 1. $\frac{1}{80}$ 2. $\frac{1}{63}$ 3. $\frac{4}{25}$ 4. $\frac{11}{9}$ or $1\frac{2}{9}$ 5. $\frac{10}{21}$ 6. $\frac{5}{6}$ 7. $\frac{6}{529}$ 8. $\frac{24}{5}$ or $4\frac{4}{5}$ 9. $\frac{1}{9}$ 10. $\frac{45}{4}$ or $11\frac{1}{4}$ 11. $\frac{1}{6}$ 12. $\frac{1}{15}$

Page 59 1. $\frac{2}{5}$ 2. $\frac{3}{4}$ 3. $\frac{1}{16}$ 4. $\frac{1}{21}$ 5. $\frac{49}{120}$ 6. $\frac{159}{272}$ 7. $\frac{30}{341}$ 8. $\frac{13}{3}$ or $4\frac{1}{3}$ 9. $\frac{1}{4}$ 10. 8 11. 2 12. $\frac{56}{25}$ or $2\frac{6}{25}$

Page 60 1. $\frac{1}{12}$ 2. $\frac{2}{91}$ 3. $\frac{27}{350}$ 4. $\frac{3}{88}$ 5. $\frac{10}{91}$ 6. $\frac{8}{81}$ 7. $\frac{28}{81}$ 8. $\frac{32}{9}$ or $3\frac{5}{9}$ 9. $\frac{8}{135}$ 10. 10 11. 52 12. $\frac{9}{4}$ or $2\frac{1}{4}$

Page 61 1. 4 2. $\frac{11}{12}$ 3. 15 4. $\frac{1}{21}$ 5. 1 6. $\frac{2}{3}$ 7. $\frac{15}{14}$ or $1\frac{1}{14}$ 8. $\frac{7}{4}$ or $1\frac{3}{4}$ 9. $\frac{45}{1196}$ 10. 1 11. 8 12. 32

Page 62 1. $\frac{3}{4}$ 2. $\frac{3}{35}$ 3. 7 4. 1 5. $\frac{5}{9}$ 6. $\frac{1}{25}$ 7. $\frac{9}{5}$ or $1\frac{4}{5}$ 8. $\frac{1}{28}$ 9. $\frac{4}{5}$ 10. $\frac{7}{16}$ 11. $\frac{2}{7}$ 12. $\frac{36}{41}$

Page 63 1. $\frac{5}{3}$ or $1\frac{2}{3}$ 2. $\frac{2}{9}$ 3. $\frac{1}{2}$ 4. $\frac{32}{99}$ 5. $\frac{7}{22}$ 6. $\frac{3}{40}$ 7. $\frac{20}{27}$ 8. $\frac{1}{24}$ 9. $\frac{6}{5}$ or $1\frac{1}{5}$ 10. $\frac{3}{8}$ 11. $\frac{7}{2}$ or $3\frac{1}{2}$ 12. $\frac{4}{17}$

Page 64 1. $\frac{2}{3}$ 2. $\frac{10}{7}$ or $1\frac{3}{7}$ 3. $\frac{1}{8}$ 4. 2 5. $\frac{16}{3}$ or $5\frac{1}{3}$ 6. $\frac{16}{15}$ or $1\frac{1}{15}$ 7. $\frac{21}{20}$ or $1\frac{1}{20}$ 8. 10 9. $\frac{45}{32}$ or $1\frac{13}{32}$ 10. $\frac{1}{3}$ 11. $\frac{5}{6}$ 12. $\frac{15}{2}$ or $7\frac{1}{2}$

Page 65 1. $\frac{22}{39}$ 2. $\frac{44}{21}$ or $2\frac{2}{21}$ 3. $\frac{83}{80}$ or $1\frac{3}{80}$ 4. $\frac{1}{3}$ 5. $\frac{3}{8}$ 6. $\frac{9}{80}$ 7. $\frac{1}{12}$ 8. $\frac{2}{91}$ 9. $\frac{9}{70}$ 10. $\frac{2}{5}$ 11. $\frac{64}{45}$ or $1\frac{19}{45}$ 12. $\frac{80}{63}$ or $1\frac{17}{63}$

Page 66 1. $\frac{20}{17}$ or $1\frac{3}{17}$ 2. $\frac{22}{15}$ or $1\frac{7}{15}$ 3. $\frac{83}{80}$ or $1\frac{3}{80}$ 4. $\frac{1}{20}$ 5. $\frac{11}{24}$ 6. $\frac{9}{32}$ 7. $\frac{3}{88}$ 8. $\frac{8}{21}$ 9. $\frac{8}{81}$ 10. $\frac{17}{18}$ 11. $\frac{4}{9}$ 12. $\frac{4}{15}$

Page 67 1. $\frac{92}{95}$ 2. $\frac{79}{48}$ or $1\frac{31}{48}$ 3. $\frac{31}{24}$ or $1\frac{7}{24}$ 4. $\frac{19}{80}$ 5. $\frac{5}{24}$ 6. $\frac{11}{48}$ 7. $\frac{28}{81}$ 8. $\frac{8}{135}$ 9. $\frac{32}{9}$ or $3\frac{5}{9}$ 10. $\frac{4}{7}$ 11. $\frac{80}{7}$ or $11\frac{3}{7}$ 12. $\frac{7}{6}$ or $1\frac{1}{6}$

Page 68 1. $\frac{221}{441}$ 2. $\frac{24}{17}$ or $1\frac{7}{17}$ 3. $\frac{89}{140}$ 4. $\frac{1}{60}$ 5. $\frac{9}{16}$ 6. $\frac{1}{6}$ 7. $\frac{1}{18}$ 8. $\frac{5}{72}$ 9. $\frac{2}{99}$ 10. $\frac{3}{4}$ 11. $\frac{9}{55}$ 12. $\frac{13}{6}$ or $2\frac{1}{6}$

Page 69 1. $13\frac{23}{30}$ 2. $4\frac{5}{6}$ 3. $3\frac{9}{32}$ 4. $16\frac{49}{60}$ 5. $9\frac{7}{12}$ 6. $14\frac{4}{9}$ 7. $12\frac{5}{16}$ 8. $7\frac{3}{10}$ 9. $16\frac{3}{4}$ 10. $8\frac{17}{30}$ 11. $16\frac{2}{5}$ 12. $8\frac{3}{14}$

Page 70 1. $5\frac{5}{8}$ 2. $20\frac{13}{36}$ 3. $18\frac{3}{8}$ 4. $18\frac{1}{28}$ 5. $10\frac{31}{36}$ 6. $12\frac{19}{20}$ 7. $11\frac{1}{80}$ 8. $19\frac{5}{51}$ 9. $16\frac{1}{12}$ 10. $14\frac{1}{10}$ 11. $10\frac{2}{15}$ 12. $12\frac{7}{10}$

Page 71 1. $5\frac{7}{40}$ 2. $7\frac{29}{40}$ 3. $11\frac{1}{8}$ 4. $12\frac{5}{16}$ 5. $15\frac{7}{40}$ 6. $10\frac{3}{4}$ 7. $29\frac{25}{48}$ 8. $11\frac{1}{32}$ 9. $14\frac{1}{3}$ 10. $13\frac{23}{30}$ 11. $42\frac{11}{30}$ 12. $14\frac{1}{4}$

Page 72 1. $16\frac{1}{2}$ 2. $8\frac{5}{8}$ 3. $15\frac{31}{48}$ 4. $6\frac{2}{3}$ 5. $3\frac{4}{5}$ 6. $9\frac{17}{18}$ 7. $25\frac{3}{4}$ 8. $28\frac{29}{40}$ 9. $7\frac{3}{100}$ 10. $16\frac{3}{5}$ 11. $4\frac{11}{16}$ 12. $12\frac{4}{15}$

Page 73   1. $5\frac{3}{8}$ 2. $20\frac{1}{4}$ 3. $1\frac{1}{2}$ 4. $2\frac{1}{4}$ 5. $8\frac{3}{16}$ 6. $3\frac{9}{16}$ 7. $1\frac{5}{12}$ 8. $2\frac{3}{8}$ 9. $2\frac{1}{16}$ 10. 35 11. $8\frac{23}{40}$ 12. $3\frac{1}{6}$

Page 74   1. $6\frac{17}{48}$ 2. $7\frac{5}{8}$ 3. $6\frac{5}{16}$ 4. $3\frac{5}{6}$ 5. $5\frac{5}{8}$ 6. $2\frac{5}{16}$ 7. $1\frac{5}{12}$ 8. $5\frac{29}{32}$ 9. $2\frac{3}{8}$ 10. $2\frac{23}{30}$ 11. $3\frac{5}{12}$ 12. $8\frac{1}{6}$

Page 75   1. $\frac{1}{4}$ 2. $2\frac{7}{20}$ 3. $10\frac{1}{8}$ 4. $7\frac{7}{8}$ 5. $9\frac{7}{36}$ 6. $1\frac{11}{12}$ 7. $\frac{3}{8}$ 8. $3\frac{13}{20}$ 9. $2\frac{5}{12}$ 10. $1\frac{7}{12}$ 11. $2\frac{3}{4}$ 12. $5\frac{1}{10}$

Page 76   1. $13\frac{2}{15}$ 2. $34\frac{5}{6}$ 3. $7\frac{1}{16}$ 4. $\frac{23}{40}$ 5. $5\frac{1}{10}$ 6. $\frac{5}{6}$ 7. $1\frac{1}{15}$ 8. $3\frac{11}{24}$ 9. $11\frac{7}{8}$ 10. $19\frac{3}{4}$ 11. $1\frac{7}{8}$ 12. $3\frac{1}{6}$

Page 77   1. $13\frac{13}{15}$ 2. 20 3. 6 4. $16\frac{1}{24}$ 5. $6\frac{1}{4}$ 6. $56\frac{1}{4}$ 7. 33 8. $7\frac{5}{7}$ 9. 35 10. 21 11. $72\frac{25}{48}$ 12. 35

Page 78   1. $7\frac{1}{5}$ 2. $9\frac{7}{12}$ 3. 18 4. 24 5. $41\frac{1}{7}$ 6. $81\frac{2}{3}$ 7. $10\frac{1}{16}$ 8. $36\frac{2}{3}$ 9. $23\frac{1}{5}$ 10. 8 11. 8 12. $\frac{1}{2}$

Page 79   1. $56\frac{1}{4}$ 2. 6 3. $26\frac{23}{48}$ 4. 16 5. $2\frac{2}{3}$ 6. 6 7. 35 8. 21 9. 60 10. $22\frac{1}{2}$ 11. $9\frac{7}{9}$ 12. 24

Page 80   1. $9\frac{1}{15}$ 2. 65 3. 16 4. 18 5. 6 6. 12 7. $2\frac{2}{3}$ 8. 63 9. $104\frac{1}{6}$ 10. 4 11. 51 12. 27

Page 81   1. $\frac{24}{49}$ 2. $2\frac{1}{2}$ 3. $2\frac{3}{5}$ 4. 20 5. $1\frac{1}{5}$ 6. $\frac{25}{54}$ 7. 7 8. $1\frac{1}{4}$ 9. $\frac{5}{7}$ 10. 2 11. 6 12. $\frac{52}{77}$

Page 82   1. $\frac{3}{4}$ 2. $\frac{2}{3}$ 3. $\frac{5}{6}$ 4. $8\frac{1}{2}$ 5. 2 6. 4 7. $1\frac{7}{18}$ 8. $2\frac{1}{2}$ 9. 8 10. $\frac{56}{75}$ 11. $2\frac{33}{50}$ 12. $\frac{2}{5}$

Page 83   1. $1\frac{1}{5}$ 2. $1\frac{1}{3}$ 3. $\frac{40}{63}$ 4. 2 5. $1\frac{8}{27}$ 6. $1\frac{25}{52}$ 7. $\frac{1}{6}$ 8. 1 9. 3 10. $\frac{18}{49}$ 11. $1\frac{3}{4}$ 12. $\frac{15}{58}$

Page 84   1. $\frac{1}{6}$ 2. 2 3. 4 4. $4\frac{1}{5}$ 5. $2\frac{1}{7}$ 6. $1\frac{1}{3}$ 7. $\frac{1}{2}$ 8. $\frac{1}{4}$ 9. $\frac{135}{196}$ 10. $4\frac{10}{11}$ 11. $1\frac{25}{26}$ 12. $3\frac{1}{2}$

Page 85   1. $6\frac{3}{8}$ 2. $7\frac{1}{3}$ 3. $17\frac{1}{16}$ 4. $4\frac{1}{2}$ 5. $5\frac{1}{6}$ 6. $6\frac{1}{2}$ 7. 111 8. 27 9. 25 10. $1\frac{1}{7}$ 11. 24 12. $3\frac{1}{16}$

Page 86   1. $42\frac{21}{40}$ 2. $15\frac{11}{24}$ 3. $10\frac{13}{30}$ 4. $18\frac{19}{24}$ 5. $3\frac{7}{16}$ 6. $6\frac{37}{80}$ 7. $6\frac{3}{10}$ 8. $5\frac{1}{32}$ 9. $31\frac{1}{2}$ 10. $2\frac{32}{33}$ 11. 4 12. $1\frac{1}{2}$

Page 87   1. $48\frac{7}{48}$ 2. $74\frac{35}{48}$ 3. $12\frac{43}{60}$ 4. $5\frac{5}{6}$ 5. $5\frac{43}{48}$ 6. $24\frac{13}{20}$ 7. $11\frac{55}{64}$ 8. $6\frac{37}{48}$ 9. $22\frac{3}{4}$ 10. $\frac{75}{88}$ 11. 20 12. $\frac{5}{8}$

Page 88   1. $19\frac{4}{9}$ 2. $32\frac{9}{16}$ 3. $23\frac{11}{24}$ 4. $12\frac{11}{35}$ 5. $5\frac{7}{12}$ 6. $8\frac{11}{24}$ 7. 5 8. $15\frac{9}{40}$ 9. $7\frac{1}{5}$ 10. 7 11. $\frac{6}{7}$ 12. $1\frac{19}{33}$

Page 89   1. $49\frac{3}{4}$ 2. $73\frac{1}{2}$ miles 3. $2\frac{1}{4}$ in. 4. $1\frac{23}{24}$ miles 5. $1\frac{1}{4}$ 6. $2\frac{2}{3}$ 7. 22 8. $5\frac{1}{2}$ ft

Page 90   1. $127\frac{31}{48}$ 2. $13\frac{3}{4}$ 3. $1\frac{3}{8}$ 4. $\frac{5}{8}$ 5. $\frac{3}{4}$ mile 6. $1\frac{25}{32}$ miles 7. $30\frac{1}{2}$ 8. $1\frac{4}{9}$ ft

Page 91   1. $60\frac{7}{8}$ miles 2. $12\frac{7}{8}$ 3. $1\frac{7}{8}$ in. 4. $\frac{9}{16}$ mile 5. $\frac{13}{14}$ 6. $13\frac{1}{2}$ cups 7. $31\frac{1}{2}$ 8. $1\frac{5}{6}$ yd

Page 92   1. $128\frac{1}{8}$ 2. $575\frac{7}{16}$ lb; no 3. $\frac{5}{8}$ 4. $1\frac{5}{8}$ ft 5. $\frac{7}{8}$ mile 6. $2\frac{1}{4}$ cups 7. $51\frac{1}{5}$ 8. $1\frac{11}{20}$ yd

Page 93   1. three thousand, two hundred seventeen 2. fourty-three and eight hundred twenty-one thousandths 3. 70,055 4. 300.122 5. $0.\overline{3}$ 6. 0.625 7. $\frac{11}{25}$ 8. $9\frac{173}{200}$ or $\frac{1973}{200}$ 9. 3800 10. 56.44 11. 63,000 12. 434.2

Page 94   1. four thousand, three hundred seventy-nine 2. four hundred seventy-six and eighty-three thousandths 3. 894,026 4. 622.37 5. $0.\overline{27}$ 6. 0.875 7. $\frac{17}{25}$ 8. $7\frac{381}{500}$ or $\frac{3881}{500}$ 9. 8600 10. 68.64 11. 890,000 12. 11.4

Page 95   1. fifty-nine thousand, six hundred forty-seven 2. eight thousand, six hundred seventy-four and ninety-three hundredths 3. 97,066 4. 202.098 5. $0.\overline{714285}$ 6. $0.8\overline{3}$ 7. $\frac{47}{50}$ 8. $5\frac{153}{200}$ or $\frac{1153}{200}$ 9. 55,000 10. 543.8 11. 8000 12. 474

Page 96   1. nine thousand, eight hundred sixty-four 2. five hundred seventy-four and eight hundred seven thousandths 3. 9602.08 4. 500,000.005 5. $0.\overline{8}$ 6. 0.9375 7. $\frac{17}{25}$ 8. $4\frac{381}{500}$ or $\frac{2381}{500}$ 9. 98.4 10. 650 11. 800 12. 89.44

Page 97   1. 72.3 2. 1.007 3. 82.371 4. 27.887 5. 70.246 6. 23.6782 7. 64.385 8. 34.8607 9. 268.6884 10. 198.5021 11. 363.88 12. 382.702

Page 98   1. 46 2. 1.3989 3. 163.9987 4. 29.6526 5. 51.026 6. 83.6759 7. 70.893 8. 104.3906 9. 195.5999 10. 187.1496 11. 66.56 12. 552.131

Page 99   1. 12.4 2. 1.3874 3. 150.15 4. 23.003 5. 65.036 6. 42.9993 7. 50.88 8. 10.8205 9. 280.7317 10. 168.2426 11. 74.84 12. 358.03

Page 100   1. 142.95 2. 0.00012 3. 58.3 4. 551.694 5. 102.12 6. 539.91 7. 597.3 8. 100.626 9. 203.124 10. 193.392 11. 13.207 12. 69.7462

Page 101   1. 8788.35 2. 857.44 3. 197.927 4. 755.6 5. 27.8803 6. 19.029 7. 2412.37 8. 153.982 9. 1816.25 10. 79.685 11. 8.922 12. 2938.23

Page 102   1. 45.02473 2. 0.132818 3. 74.786 4. 79.86995 5. 6.5428 6. 20.6712 7. 274.975 8. 27.89379 9. 47.77 10. 1.0478 11. 32.4761 12. 152.7065

Page 103   1. 185.69 2. 45.096 3. 0.52685 4. 100.617 5. 32,297.037 6. 1.5788 7. 28.726 8. 20.3348 9. 35.562 10. 233.544 11. 1490.784 12. 13,401.507

Page 104   1. 7588.27 2. 380.98 3. 169.965 4. 867.8 5. 39.8608 6. 4.079 7. 1123.07 8. 130.975 9. 1415.17 10. 7.311 11. 2610.13 12. 42,022.221

Page 105   1. 15.078 2. 100.45 3. 0.11418 4. 594 5. 5.0662 6. 35.14 7. 678.6 8. 3.492 9. 44.4577 10. 352.88 11. 0.168 12. 4282.18

Page 106   1. 10.191 2. 157.92 3. 0.07612 4. 680.36 5. 3.8761 6. 15.96672 7. 73.47 8. 1.416 9. 6.0576 10. 298.98 11. 0.3995 12. 3.78176

Page 107   1. 22.512 2. 13.832 3. 0.136032 4. 2086 5. 1.61393 6. 17.1174 7. 748.8 8. 466.52 9. 19.8288 10. 1079.5 11. 0.21162 12. 3650

Page 108 1. 17.064 2. 18.3114 3. 152.5533 4. 9391.36 5. 28.8123 6. 847.705 7. 600.502 8. 2062.83 9. 97.137 10. 27.767 11. 0.0243872 12. 408.58

Page 109 1. 0.0902 2. 62.57 3. 15.36 4. 0.125 5. 0.13747 6. 14.5 7. 8.72 8. 440 9. 0.4375 10. 15.8 11. 1.654 12. 15.63

Page 110 1. 0.0601 2. 2.31 3. 6.541 4. 0.375 5. 0.13679 6. 25.7 7. 65.41 8. 120 9. 0.3125 10. 12.67 11. 0.1739 12. 17.83

Page 111 1. 0.0701 2. 39.5 3. 7.94 4. 0.875 5. 0.07787 6. 10.8 7. 46.5 8. 160 9. 0.5625 10. 53.6 11. 0.804 12. 387.5

Page 112 1. 0.068 2. 40.6 3. 10.203 4. 0.625 5. 200.1 6. 16,717 7. 205 8. 200 9. 0.6875 10. 910.04 11. 834 12. 400

Page 113 1. 9666.83 2. 1156.6756 3. 900.733 4. 375.919 5. 823.89 6. 838.703 7. 6.491394 8. 2951.975664 9. 212.861 10. 9.55 11. 2.011 12. 91.2

Page 114 1. 820.4839 2. 510.4123 3. 198.17 4. 22.6939 5. 455.37 6. 709.039 7. 177.71008 8. 1229.307072 9. 64.1586 10. 6.45 11. 3.012 12. 65.4

Page 115 1. 49.3875 2. 879.909 3. 7151.23 4. 677.882 5. 2.885 6. 688.405 7. 9.3126795 8. 53,894.463 9. 833.4128 10. 7.12 11. 2.001 12. 76.2

Page 116 1. 62.3843 2. 998.076 3. 1085.825 4. 878.341 5. 31.102 6. 782.168 7. 12.41955 8. 59,841.6135 9. 761.392 10. 8.15 11. 1.059 12. 83.2

Page 117 1. $620.26 2. $8515.20 3. 100,000 4. $13,288.71 5. 11,894.217 6. 4.02 in. 7. 2898 cm³ 8. $3013.85

Page 118 1. 7.48 2. $379.72 3. 131.25 oz 4. 22.67 5. 13,095.015 miles 6. $1450.68 7. 9.8 lb 8. 8.5

Page 119 1. $97.34 2. $1900.81 3. $467.46 4. 741 people 5. 3684.79 cm³ 6. 7584.752 7. 73.78 miles 8. 1.46 mi²

Page 120 1. $398.65 2. $5.55 3. $2891.89 4. $144.35 5. $3386.90 6. 560.56 miles 7. 12.13 miles 8. 0.007 mi²

Page 121 1. 80% 2. 50% 3. 62% 4. 0.4% 5. 62.5% 6. 13.86 7. 0.052 8. 76 9. $\frac{18}{25}$ 10. 33 11. 6.48 12. $66\frac{2}{3}$%

Page 122 1. 3.5% 2. 10.88 3. 0.31% 4. 75% 5. $\frac{21}{25}$ 6. 1.472 7. 87.5% 8. 120% 9. 57% 10. 60 11. 1750% 12. 37.5%

Page 123 1. 40% 2. 0.0016 3. 80% 4. 10.71 5. 0.51% 6. 24 7. 108 8. 40% 9. 13 10. 20% 11. 76% 12. 25%

Page 124 1. 25% 2. 29% 3. 0.43 4. 30% 5. 20% 6. 5.25 7. 27 8. 63 9. 20% 10. 57% 11. 6.396 12. 20%

Page 125 1. 27 2. 83 3. 16% 4. $66 5. 30% 6. $450 7. $30 8. $1000 9. $120 10. $56,000

Page 126 1. 62 2. 87 3. 42% 4. $108.50 5. $300 6. 20% 7. $40 8. $1500 9. $135 10. $84,750

Page 127 1. 33 2. 72 3. 45% 4. $123 5. $12\frac{1}{2}$ 6. $42 7. $288 8. $2200 9. $108 10. $94,500

Page 128 1. 64 2. 103 3. 51% 4. $112.50 5. $33\frac{1}{3}$% 6. 473 7. $56 8. $2000 9. $131.25 10. $1,035,000

Page 129 1. 113 2. −10 3. 194 4. 240 5. 6 6. 60 7. 18 8. 45 9. 540 10. 1400 11. 3520 12. 204

Page 130 1. 68 2. 45 3. 176 4. 84 5. 17 6. 16 7. 4700 8. 26,000 9. 30.1 10. 32,000 11. 5.20 12. 17,000

Page 131 1. 95 2. 60 3. 10 4. 11 5. 300 6. 144 7. 52 8. 15,840 9. 1236 10. 14 11. 141 12. 5280

Page 132 1. 140 2. 50 3. 65 4. 15 5. 52 6. 15 7. 47,000 8. 6.152 9. 0.00083 10. 5.9 11. 0.0635 12. 0.082

Page 133 1. 120° 2. 49° 3. 47°, 63°, 70° 4. 36°, 100°, 44° 5. 60°, 100°, 110°, 90° 6. 53°, 60°, 67°

Page 134 1. 122° 2. 70° 3. 52°, 88°, 40° 4. 90°, 32°, 58° 5. 44°, 105°, 31° 6. 88°, 77°, 80°, 115°

Page 135 1. 70° 2. 105° 3. 55°, 75°, 50° 4. 43°, 90°, 47° 5. 80°, 86°, 106°, 88° 6. 22°, 141°, 17°

Page 136 1. 138° 2. 70° 3. 68°, 30°, 82° 4. 27°, 103°, 50° 5. 48°, 81°, 51° 6. 89°, 83°, 88°, 100°

Page 137 1. $3\frac{1}{8}$ in.², $7\frac{1}{2}$ in. 2. 2 yd², 6 yd 3. 5 ft², 9 ft 4. $12\frac{1}{4}$ in.², 14 in. 5. $2\frac{13}{16}$ mi², 7 mi

Page 138 1. 3.75 m², 8 m 2. 2.25 km², 6.5 km 3. 3.0625 dm², 7 dm 4. 5.3125 m², 11 m 5. 7.875 cm², 13.5 cm

Page 139 1. $3\frac{1}{8}$ in.², $7\frac{1}{2}$ in. 2. $5\frac{1}{2}$ mi², $9\frac{1}{2}$ mi 3. $4\frac{1}{2}$ ft², 9 ft 4. $4\frac{7}{8}$ yd², $9\frac{1}{2}$ yd 5. 3 in.², $9\frac{1}{2}$ in.

Page 140 1. 4.375 km², 8.5 km 2. 2.5 dm², 6.5 km 3. 8.4375 m², 12 m 4. 3.5 km², 7.8 km 5. 4.25 cm², 10.5 cm

Page 141 1. $1\frac{1}{4}$ in., 3 in., $3\frac{1}{4}$ in., $1\frac{1}{4}$ in., $1\frac{7}{8}$ in.², $7\frac{1}{2}$ in. 2. $1\frac{3}{4}$ in., $3\frac{1}{2}$ in., $1\frac{3}{4}$ in., 2 in., $1\frac{1}{2}$ in., $4\frac{1}{8}$ in.², 9 in. 3. $1\frac{1}{2}$ in., $2\frac{1}{2}$ in., $1\frac{1}{2}$ in., $3\frac{3}{4}$ in.², 8 in.

Page 142 1. 41 mm, 51 mm, 48 mm, 36 mm, 918 mm², 140 mm 2. 39 mm, 70 mm, 38 mm, 2660 mm², 218 mm 3. 43 mm, 72 mm, 48 mm, 45 mm, 43 mm, 2515.5 mm², 208 mm

Page 143 1. $1\frac{1}{4}$ in., $3\frac{3}{4}$ in., $1\frac{1}{2}$ in., $5\frac{5}{8}$ in.², 10 in. 2. $2\frac{1}{2}$ in., $3\frac{1}{2}$ in., 2 in., $1\frac{1}{2}$ in., $2\frac{5}{8}$ in.², 8 in. 3. 2 in., $4\frac{1}{4}$ in., 2 in., 2 in., $1\frac{3}{4}$ in., $5\frac{15}{32}$ in.², $10\frac{1}{4}$ in.

216

Page 144   **1.** 43 mm, 90 mm, 68 mm, 32 mm, 1440 mm², 201 mm **2.** 39 mm, 59 mm, 38 mm, 2242 mm², 196 mm **3.** 40 mm, 77 mm, 44 mm, 51 mm, 39 mm, 2496 mm², 212 mm

Page 145   **1.** 343 in.³ **2.** 5525 ft³ **3.** 325 in.³ **4.** 381,510 ft³ **5.** 58,944.08 in.³ **6.** 2,001,750 in.³

Page 146   **1.** 2197 cm³ **2.** 816 mm³ **3.** 1140 cm³ **4.** 38,772.72 m³ **5.** 7385.28 cm³ **6.** 10,562.96 mm³

Page 147   **1.** 1331 in.³ **2.** 432 ft³ **3.** 10,500 in.³ **4.** $179,503\frac{1}{3}$ in.³ **5.** 155,090.88 yd³ **6.** 67,852.26 in.³

Page 148   **1.** 512 mm³ **2.** 6160 cm³ **3.** 539 m³ **4.** 113,040 cm³ **5.** 22,155.84 cm³ **6.** 4019.2 m³

Page 149   **1.** 25 in., 157 in., 1962.5 in.² **2.** 19 ft, 119.32 ft, 1133.54 ft² **3.** 2 yd, 12.56 yd, 12.56 yd² **4.** 15 ft, 94.2 ft, 706.5 ft² **5.** 7.5 in., 47.1 in., 176.625 in.²

Page 150   **1.** 17 mm, 106.76 mm, 907.46 mm² **2.** 20 cm, 125.6 cm, 1256 cm² **3.** 10 dm, 62.8 dm, 314 dm² **4.** 15 m, 94.2 m, 706.5 m² **5.** 9.5 cm, 59.66 cm, 283.385 cm²

Page 151   **1.** 25 yd, 157 yd, 1962.5 yd² **2.** 16 in., 100.48 in., 803.84 in.² **3.** 9 ft, 56.52 ft, 254.34 ft² **4.** 26 in., 163.28 in., 2122.64 in.² **5.** 22.5 ft, 141.3 ft, 1589.625 ft²

Page 152   **1.** 2.5 km, 15.7 km, 19.625 km² **2.** 30 mm, 188.4 mm, 2826 mm² **3.** 7 dm, 43.96 dm, 153.86 dm² **4.** 38 cm, 238.64 cm, 4534.16 cm² **5.** 15 m, 94.2 m, 706.5 m²

Page 153   **1.** 1 $10, 1 25¢, 3 1¢ **2.** 3 $1, 1 10¢, 1 5¢, 4 1¢ **3.** 1 $5, 2 $1, 2 $1, 1 25¢, 1 10¢, 1 5¢, 3 1¢ **4.** 1 $10, 1 $1, 1 50¢, 1 10¢, 1 5¢, 3 1¢ **5.** 1 $10, 4 $1, 1 50¢, 1 25¢, 1 5¢, 4 1¢ **6.** 1 $10, 2 $1, 2 10¢, 2 1¢ **7.** c **8.** c **9.** b **10.** a **11.** c **12.** c

Page 154   **1.** 1 $10, 2 $1, 1 50¢, 1 10¢, 1 5¢, 3 1¢ **2.** 4 $1, 1 25¢, 1 10¢, 1 5¢, 3 1¢ **3.** 1 $5, 2 $1, 1 25¢, 1 10¢, 1 5¢, 1 1¢ **4.** 1 $10, 1 $5, 1 $1, 1 25¢, 1 5¢, 2 1¢ **5.** 1 $10, 1 10¢, 1 5¢, 2 1¢ **6.** 1 $10, 2 $1 3, 1¢ **7.** b **8.** c **9.** a **10.** a **11.** c **12.** b

Page 155   **1.** 1 $5, 2 $1, 1 25¢, 1 10¢, 1 5¢, 1 1¢ **2.** 1 $10, 2 $1, 1 10¢, 1 5¢, 2 1¢ **3.** 3 $1, 1 50¢, 2 1¢ **4.** 1 $10, 1 $5, 1 50¢, 1 25¢, 2 10¢, 1 5¢, 3 1¢ **5.** 1 $10, 1 $1, 1 50¢, 1 10¢, 1 5¢, 3 1¢ **6.** 1 $5, 1 10¢, 1 5¢, 4 1¢ **7.** a **8.** c **9.** c **10.** c **11.** b **12.** a

Page 156   **1.** 1 $5, 3 $1, 1 25¢, 1 10¢, 1 5¢, 2 1¢ **2.** 1 $5, 1 $1, 1 50¢, 1 10¢, 1 5¢, 3 1¢ **3.** 2 $1, 1 10¢, 1 5¢, 3 1¢ **4.** 1 $10, 1 50¢, 2 10¢, 2 1¢ **5.** 1 $10, 2 $1, 1 10¢, 1 5¢ **6.** 1 $10, 1 25¢, 1 10¢, 4 1¢ **7.** b **8.** a **9.** c **10.** c **11.** b **12.** c

Page 157   **1.** 12% **2.** 288 **3.** $102\frac{2}{3}$ **4.** $6803\frac{1}{3}$ **5.** $2.23 **6.** 13.9

Page 158   **1.** 49% **2.** 51 **3.** $108.01 **4.** $126.75 **5.** $109,949 **6.** $198

Page 159   **1.** 3.08 sec **2.** 1.6 mph **3.** 174 liters **4.** 14% **5.** $11.13 **6.** $9492.25

Page 160 **1.** 80.2 **2.** $337.12 **3.** $70.08 **4.** $5625 **5.** $58 **6.** 5¢

Pages 161-173   **1.** C **2.** A **3.** A **4.** C **5.** A **6.** A **7.** D **8.** B **9.** D **10.** B **11.** C **12.** D **13.** B **14.** D **15.** A **16.** A **17.** B **18.** D **19.** C **20.** C **21.** A **22.** B **23.** D **24.** D **25.** C **26.** B **27.** C **28.** B **29.** B **30.** D **31.** C **32.** D **33.** C **34.** D **35.** C **36.** D **37.** A **38.** D **39.** A **40.** B **41.** A **42.** D **43.** B **44.** A **45.** D **46.** D **47.** D **48.** A **49.** B **50.** C **51.** B **52.** D **53.** B **54.** C **55.** A **56.** D **57.** C **58.** B **59.** B **60.** D **61.** C **62.** C **63.** D **64.** A **65.** A **66.** A **67.** B **68.** C **69.** A **70.** B **71.** B **72.** D **73.** C **74.** C **75.** D **76.** C **77.** A **78.** B **79.** A **80.** A **81.** C **82.** C **83.** B **84.** B **85.** A **86.** B **87.** A **88.** C **89.** D **90.** B **91.** A **92.** A **93.** A **94.** B **95.** C **96.** D **97.** C **98.** B **99.** D **100.** C

Pages 174-186   **1.** C **2.** A **3.** C **4.** A **5.** A **6.** B **7.** C **8.** A **9.** D **10.** D **11.** B **12.** D **13.** C **14.** A **15.** B **16.** C **17.** C **18.** B **19.** A **20.** D **21.** A **22.** D **23.** D **24.** B **25.** B **26.** C **27.** D **28.** A **29.** C **30.** D **31.** D **32.** D **33.** C **34.** B **35.** D **36.** A **37.** C **38.** A **39.** A **40.** C **41.** D **42.** B **43.** B **44.** A **45.** D **46.** B **47.** C **48.** D **49.** B **50.** A **51.** B **52.** B **53.** C **54.** D **55.** C **56.** B **57.** B **58.** C **59.** A **60.** B **61.** C **62.** C **63.** D **64.** C **65.** D **66.** B **67.** D **68.** A **69.** A **70.** B **71.** B **72.** A **73.** A **74.** A **75.** C **76.** A **77.** B **78.** D **79.** B **80.** D **81.** A **82.** B **83.** A **84.** C **85.** B **86.**   **87.** C **88.** B **89.** D **90.** C **91.** A **92.** D **93.** A **94.** B **95.** D **96.** A **97.** A **98.** B **99.** C **100.** C

Pages 187-199   **1.** D **2.** A **3.** B **4.** C **5.** C **6.** B **7.** A **8.** C **9.** D **10.** B **11.** D **12.** D **13.** A **14.** C **15.** B **16.** A **17.** A **18.** C **19.** A **20.** C **21.** C **22.** A **23.** A **24.** C **25.** A **26.** D **27.** B **28.** C **29.** D **30.** D **31.** D **32.** C **33.** A **34.** D **35.** C **36.** B **37.** B **38.** D **39.** D **40.** A **41.** B **42.** A **43.** C **44.** B **45.** B **46.** C **47.** B **48.** C **49.** D **50.** B **51.** A **52.** B **53.** D **54.** C **55.** B **56.** D **57.** A **58.** B **59.** B **60.** D **61.** D **62.** B **63.** D **64.** B **65.** A **66.** C **67.** A **68.** C **69.** B **70.** C **71.** B **72.** A **73.** A **74.** B **75.** C **76.** D **77.** D **78.** D **79.** D **80.** C **81.** C **82.** C **83.** B **84.** A **85.** A **86.** D **87.** B **88.** A **89.** D **90.** A **91.** C **92.** D **93.** B **94.** C **95.** D **96.** C **97.** C **98.** A **99.** B **100.** A

Pages 200-212   **1.** D **2.** C **3.** B **4.** D **5.** C **6.** A **7.** A **8.** A **9.** B **10.** D **11.** B **12.** A **13.** C **14.** D **15.** B **16.** C **17.** C **18.** B **19.** B **20.** A **21.** C **22.** A **23.** B **2.** A **25.** A **26.** B **27.** D **28.** C **29.** C **30.** D **31.** A **32.** B **33.** B **34.** A **35.** B **36.**   **37.** C **38.** C **39.** A **40.** A **41.** D **42.** D **43.** D **44.** B **45.** D **46.** B **47.** D **48.** B **49.** C **50.** A **51.** D **52.** D **53.** A **54.** B **55.** C **56.** D **57.** C **58.** B **59.** A **60.** D **61.** A **62.** A **63.** D **64.** A **65.** B **66.** C **67.** D **68.** C **69.** B **70.** C **71.** B **72.** C **73.** B **74.** C **75.** A **76.** D **77.** B **78.** D **79.** D **80.** C **81.** A **82.** B **83.** A **84.** D **85.** C **86.** C **87.** D **88.** B **89.** D **90.** A **91.** A **92.** D **93.** B **94.** B **95.** D **96.** C **97.** A **98.** D **99.** C **100.** A